Franz Günter Leicht

Paradigm shift towards a spiritual Worldview

General practical considerations

Volume 1

Paradigm shift towards a spiritual Worldview

General practical considerations

Franz Günter Leicht

Volume 1

Bibliographic information published by the Deutsche Nationalbibliothek. The Deutsche Nationalbibliothek lists this publication in the Deutsche Nationalbibliografie; detailed bibliographic data are available on the internet: http://dnb.dnb.de

© 2021 Franz Günter Leicht

1st Edition April 2021

Published and printed by: BoD - Books on Demand, Norderstedt/Germany

ISBN: 978-3-7534-2343-2

Content

I. Independence (consideration from a primarily materialistic perspective)

Note: This section deals with the question of the extent to which it is possible to maintain some independence despite being embedded in the collective.

1. To what extent we are independent.

Keywords.

- feeling of belonging.
- life in community
- life in isolation
- reconciliation.
- where does the force wear come from?

Below we will give simple examples to make it clear, that our life is much easier, if we are there for each other and live a life of human co-existence, than to live a life of ego trip, of individual efforts or a life against each other.

General considerations.

It is undisputed that we have each other and that we share life with one another. With some we share a house, an idea, a goal or other similarities. We share the air with each other. We share a country with each other. We share the earth with each other. We share the universe with each other. We also share things with each other that we cannot (currently) see, but which nevertheless are there.

If the social environment were not there, we could not live. We wouldn't have any problems without the world around us. We can only have problems with the other. So, we never can solve them alone, but only with the world around us. Acting separately is the wrong way to solve problems. It leads us into isolation. In isolation, life is dreary and loveless. Furthermore, in isolation there is no sense of belonging. If this is missing, life appears meaningless. Then we literally are precluding the world around us. **We think that if we open up to the outside world, we're losing our identity.** The opposite is the case, because identity always has something to do with belonging.

Someone who isolates himself completely leaves his intellectual faculties that lie dormant in him unused. Yes, his skills are wasting away. And the ones he still has are of no use to anyone. He himself is dissatisfied, only scolds the others and is obnoxious. And because he is inhibited from sheer fear, annoyance, hatred and the like to move freely in society, his freedom is significantly restricted. So, what could isolation and lack of freedom have to do with any identity? In addition, in isolation we also feel lonely and closer to death than to life. Yes, then we wish to be dead rather than alive.

On the other hand, if we open ourselves up to the outside world and show ourselves well-disposed towards everyone, the others will want to connect with us in some form. Or who is so stupid that he rejects friends and connects with enemies? Even if, despite our goodwill, someone does not want to connect with us, they still support our actions indirectly. At least they will not want to torpedo our actions. In any case, we will be able to win over a large part of the world around us. Because this part would find our actions to be good and will even accommodate our actions, this increases our scope for action. And so, we can develop our abilities that are within us. Overall, this makes us freer and more powerful.

However, if we show us to the world around us as selfish, unfair, arrogant and aggressive, it will impose us different restrictions. And precisely this reduces our scope for action and makes us unfree. If we feel unfree, we also feel like an outsider, what does not exactly give us a sense of identity.

Depending on the situation, we know different feelings of identity, which is expressed by a certain sense of belonging. So, we can't only feel that we belong to our family, but also to an association, a state, humanity, the earth's inhabitants, etc. There are no limits to our sense of belonging. Is this boundlessness justified? In a strict sense, the boundless sense of belonging is the only true feeling of belonging. Why?

As a single person, we don't live for ourselves. We live from minerals, plants, animals and ultimately from the entire environment. Without the earthly diversity, which is a rather complex interaction field, the individual earthly life forms cannot live. One form needs the other. Earth in turn needs the sun, because life on earth is not possible without the sun. Our solar system is part of our galaxy, which in turn is part of a galaxy cluster; etc.

And whether the entire visible universe can be the basis for all being and life is questionable. Finally, there are many indications that indicate that there are higher levels of being. In particular, if there are indications that indicate the existence of higher levels of being, we even have to demand the existence of the invisible. There are the religions that provide these clues. People who can reach and even perceive higher levels of being in meditation also provide clues for this. Yes, there are even scientists who say that they can prove GOD whatever that is supposed to mean by the term 'GOD'. So, we have to broaden our sense of identity if we want to show a legitimate sense of identity.

In any case, one thing is clear. The lower our identity thinking, the less free we feel. The bigger our identity thinking gets, the freer we feel. After all, it is this limitlessness that allows our spirit to look into infinity. And so, there are no real limits either in the sense of identity or in our thinking.

What practical options does this fact allow? Even if we perceive ourselves as limited, we can either win over the world or turn our backs on it. If we try to win over the world, we have more space to maneuver. But if we turn our backs on it, our scope for action becomes smaller.

We can lead separate lives even though we have each other. But what is the result? Nobody is really happy with it. If everyone is laboring on their own, there is hardly any reason to look for joy, because nobody really lets the others share in their lives. The other's opinion is not really taken seriously. It falls by the wayside. Yes, the other one falls by the wayside because he is not taken seriously.

It is obvious that this path is not really good for anyone, that it never really serves anyone, and that it is associated with a wear and tear on the strength. In this way we do something that is contrary to life. Too often we don't have strength for anything. But we could have it much easier if we only reversed the direction of the path. Common paths are always easier and more effective than a single-handedly life. It doesn't matter where we are. Even if our life seems to be ruined, we have the opportunity to raise up again. After all, people have always been able to raise up after a fall, however deep it was, or after a very serious illness.

Only physical death would make the ascent impossible. However, it is still open whether life will continue after the physical death or not. In the event that it continues, we will not be able to avoid the problem raised. Then it won't let us go. If we lead a single-handedly life, the world around us will come more out in resistance than if we try to integrate the other into our lives.

Those who completely distance themselves from the world can't progress and do not really live. On the contrary, they will face a creeping death. So why to wait so long until nothing works if we can stop now our gradual fall and turn our lives around? It's worth an attempt, isn't it?

Even if there are setbacks again and again, we can progress in the long run. Decisive for a gradual progress is not that there has to be only progresses, but that we take more steps forward than backwards. It is certainly desirable to make just progress if possible. The step backwards as such does not stop really our development, however, because it cannot really stop our choice to try again with a few more steps forward.

If we want to go this way, we look in the direction of the good, so to speak, without really having to see it. We do this exactly as we do with every goal that we strive for. This is not immediately visible, but only when we have reached it. Let us simply imagine that at the end of this goal only the good is available. At the other end there is only the bad. In between we have both the one and the other to varying degrees. And depending on where we stand, the one or the other pre-dominates.

Note: With 'good' is to be understood something that we consider desirable or which has to do with peace, with joy, with harmony, with benevolence, with success, with progress and the like. 'Bad' is to be understood as something that displeases us or what has to do with strife, disharmony, anger, struggle, malice, failure, regression and the like.

```
bad      bad    Stand-  bad          good
bad <-----bad-------*-----------good---------> good
bad      good   point   good         good
```

If we look towards the good, the way we go goes there. Then we open a kind of virtuous circle (opposite of vicious circle). Otherwise, if we look in the direction of the bad, the path leads to the bad. Then we end up in a vicious circle. This is very elementary and very easy to understand. Whether there is Good in the absolute or not does not affect here either. Because as long as there is an opportunity to do something positive, we can also take steps in this direction. We will be stopped only when we are dead. But then the question of target tracking no longer arises.

Note. When we speak of steps towards the good, steps are to be understood in terms of development forward or upward. Otherwise, the steps go back or down. We can also imagine a kind of development ladder on which we are and which we can go up and down step by step. If we climb up, we make progress in terms of development. In the other case, setbacks. As you can see, in the long run we can, so to speak, stand still, even though we have labored and have become older from a physical point of view. This is the case if we take the same number of steps forward and backward on average. The aging of the body therefore is not necessarily a measure of development. **But we want to work on the inner development.** We can view the current position, wherever it may be, as value-neutral. After all, it is not a bad thing to be in development. Furthermore, what is good for one person may not be good for another, that is, bad. Or what seemed *good to me yesterday, I can feel it as bad for me today; and vice versa. So, who can really tell if something is good or bad?*

But we still have a way to find criteria to tell whether it goes in one direction or the other. In any case, because we have each other, the connection is in the sense of life and the distancing is against life. How can we still recognize which direction it is going? Very simple: **by the inner peace**. If we e.g. have quarreled and left the situation upset, offended, hurt or with an uneasy feeling, we can be sure that we have no inner peace. Because we usually draw conclusions from such situations that make us turn our backs even more on the world, there is a greater likelihood of going backwards. If the dispute is ended with reconciliation, we have at least not achieved any strife. After a reconciled situation we are more likely to take steps towards the world around us and therefore towards the inner peace.

Generally speaking, if we go out of a situation that gives us a good feeling, we can assume that we have come a little closer to the world around us. In the other case, we distanced ourselves a little more from it. From this point of view, our path, however different it may look, always offers only two possible directions. In every situation we have the choice for one or the other direction.

So, think that it is always the path of communion that fills our lives and makes us happy. It goes without saying that letting go of a relationship, be it with a person, with an idea or with something, can free us up for other relationships so that we can get closer to the world around us. In this case we replace e.g. a less vivid relationship through a more vivid relationship. Or we replace for example a relationship that runs counter to our goals through a relationship that is consistent with our goals. Every change that we initiate in life needs (and has) an alternative.

In a sense, one relationship must die to make space for another relationship. This process of change generally also takes place in earthly life. Earthly life is preserved by killing to live. Nevertheless, it can develop as a whole or, in the reverse case, also degenerate. If we look at the development history of the earth, we can clearly see that earthly life is currently declining in diversity.

The question of who or what is responsible for this decline in species has a simple answer. It is of all the most highly developed form of being on earth, namely man, that is currently working against the further development of earthly life. And this also considers himself to be the crown of creation. In any case, there will be anything that man doesn't have understood. What the human being as a mass apparently did not understand is that community at all levels is required not only to maintain earthly life but also to keep it viable.

Whatever stands in the way of life must be given up, if possible, and what is useful for life must be pushed. Each individual is called upon to do this. There are many possibilities and opportunities. We just have to seize the opportunities. We can do this step by step. Where we are standing right now, whether at the bottom, in the middle or at the top, is unimportant. It will be impossible to avoid the change. But the direction is in our own hands. Where do you want to go?

There are many opportunities to connect with the world a little more. Because there are enough people who are lonely and looking forward to a little visit or a small conversation. There are always opportunities to help out here and there, even if it is only a small step. We can help someone across the street if they are struggling on their own. Or we can give someone a smile or just greet someone without caring whether they are younger or older. It doesn't always have to be something big. Sometimes a small gesture of approach has a big impact. Sometimes it helps the other if we show good intentions. The small in the sum also results in something big.

If we make other people happy, the joy is transmitted. So, we make ourselves a joy at the same time. We cannot be happy if we fail to do something that brings joy. After all, it's hard to be happy alone. The joy is greater for two and is also much easier to accomplish. **It is said that shared joy is double (multiple) joy.** The more people are happy about something, the greater the joy. Yes, joy can grow to an enormous enthusiasm and be really mesmerizing, which is not uncommon in football stadiums. The fascinating thing is that it is not difficult for us to get carried away. It is much more difficult to put ourselves in such enthusiasm for us alone. Yes, it is almost not possible without the surroundings (in the isolation).

The enthusiasm in the crowd is much easier for us because everyone is involved, so to speak, in resonance vibration, which is physically a more favorable state of being compared to isolated states of emotions. And an energetically more favorable state of being is also a more harmonious state. If everyone hides in their emotional world to be in the doldrums, it is as if physically seen everyone would build their own dissonance system, which is associated with increased energy expenditure. And what is associated with increased energy expenditure is in any case more strenuous. Seen in this way, for physical reasons alone, a way of 'connecting' makes our lives easier. This effect is not only limited to our emotional world.

It cannot be denied that there are many areas in life where we can contribute to make our lives either easier or harder. However, it is not necessary and perhaps not possible to find a way to make our life easier at every moment. But where it is possible, it is to be called for. In order to become more aware of this, we can take a little time to classify a typical day that we experience, on a note sheet according to such criteria. Where can we change something and where not? We can also note how much time we spend on self-pity and mental activities with things that are long gone and therefore can no longer be changed. This time is usually wasted unless we learn something from it. Therefore, we should not use the past to experience the blues, because it does not bring us anything. Instead, we can use this time for other purposes.

Now we could say that some people with whom we have a lot to do are how they are, and that they impose certain behavior on us that we can hardly avoid. If they could really impose their behavior on us, we would have to be like themselves and act like them at the same time. We would be more or less dependent on them. Are we really dependent on them? Surely not, because we always have the possibility of not exerting any counter pressure on pressure from the other or of not countering the verbal or physical violence of the other with the same or similar way.

Sometimes we will hardly want or be able to have any other choice than to counter with something similar, but sometimes we will have the choice after all. Wherever it is possible, we should not do the same to the other person unless we want to do it from our heart. Responding to good with good should not be a question in view of your own well-being. And if it is possible to respond to evil with good, neither. Because this would certainly not affect our well-being.

What if we always retaliate with similar means and make it dependent on how the other person is to us? This would be in line with the motto: *'If the other is good to me, I will also be good to him; and if the other will be bad to me, I will be bad to him too'*. Then we lay our fate in the hands of the other and make ourselves quasi dependent on him, without being really dependent on him. Yes, then we would virtually 'crawl in his butt' and even betray our principles. Do we really want to do the others this favor? We can probably think if we counter good influence on his bad influence, that we will crawl in the other's butt. Indeed, this is not the case, because we do not the same thing as the other. Because then we show him that at the moment we are different from him. In a way, we even show strength because we are doing something that is at least yet unusual today.

Besides, what use is it if we let ourselves be dragged down by others? Isn't it the case, that this will harm ourselves? Or when we get into a fight, isn't it sometimes the case that we think how stupid we were that we let ourselves down to the level of the other? Or what do we lose if we overlook the quirks of others, even if we can't stand them? If we are constantly annoyed with others, we are doing something that automatically brings us into a state of dissatisfaction. And so, we lose our inner peace.

Seen in this way, in terms of our well-being, we are primarily dependent on ourselves and less on others, which is a good thing. To confirm this, we can use the fact that our energy-body system has self-healing powers that can at least heal minor injuries. In case of major injuries, this will not be possible without further ado, but this does not necessarily mean to be dependent on the other. This would at most be the case if we come across someone out of pure coincidence or by a certain insidiousness who inflicts such an injury on us and we cannot take advantage of the possibility of protection. And then we cannot be sure whether this unexpected encounter is not also a fateful affair.

Who has not already experienced dangerous situations that have run as by a wonder a mild course and has said to himself: *'Oh, there I had a good guardian angel'*. Or someone got sick and was therefore unable to take a plane that later crashed. So, something unfortunate happened to him that ultimately meant his luck. Or someone gets a job in a company, makes a bigger move and half a year later the company goes bankrupt. Something lucky happened to him that ultimately meant his bad luck. Many examples could be put in place, which seem to turn seemingly negative as good but also seemingly good as negative.

Furthermore, it is conceivable and also possible that there is eternal life and we are therefore not really vulnerable. In this case, the body would be something like a symbol and the outside world would be something like a world of experience, a teaching or therapeutic unit, which would among other things point out a fault (failing) that may lie within ourselves. But this would not mean that the fault is not in the other too. In fact, it is more likely that we only meet because there are certain points of contact that point to a certain learning topic that is not so different from the other. In this respect, we always have to ask ourselves when we judge incomprehensible situations, whether we are correct with our judgment or not. It should be clear that we cannot understand many things. However, this does not mean that we should not question life. Everyone has the right to do this. Another question is whether this questioning brings us anything. In order to answer this question, we would have to step deeper into this topic, what we are not doing yet.

At first, we just pretend that there is no eternal life and that general events have no fate-related background. Then we initially have no other choice but to accept that we find ourselves in a world that just shows itself as it is. Even then it is possible to steer our life in a certain direction. It is not even necessary to believe in God. It is sufficient to follow the law of energy minimization in order to steer our life in the direction that is good for us.

Above we came to the conclusions that a life against each other and a life of ego-trip is harder and more exhausting than a way for each other and with each other. Those who take the first mentioned way violate the law of energy minimizing and go against life. The result is struggle, exertion and fatigue. On the other hand, life for one another and for each other suffice the energy minimalism.

No matter which direction our path will take, it will lead to a change. In doing so, we can take advantage of the fact that people are highly imitators. If I'm ruthless, I encourage the other person to be ruthless as well. If I get along well with one, it is not difficult for the other to get along well with me. Of course, there are exceptions. But these confirm the rule. If we are currently in a society in that most people mainly elbow others out of the way, on the one hand this is an indication of this imitation. On the other hand, this shows that most people choose the wrong means for their salvation. Not a few should be aware of this. Then why don't they do anything about it?

One of the main reasons is that there is a general feeling that we would drive better in life and would have an easier life if we were to swim with the flow of generality. The mass itself shows that this thinking is an error, because it is rather itself which sees itself in battle, is dissatisfied and sees the scapegoat of misery in the other. Because the struggle is inherently tiring, it does not represent the ease of being. And because the broad mass prefers to be ruthless, it does not at all decide for the lightness of being. We should all be aware that we have the ability to act both wisely or unwise. And according to what has just been said, it should be clear enough that going with the crowd obviously does not make our lives easier in the long run, does it?

Incidentally, there are people, even though they are few compared to the mass, who succeed almost everything they tackle. Why do they succeed? Perhaps they have a different outlook on life and have understood the principle of energy minimalism. In any case, they would be better off than the mass. And precisely because there are few people who exemplify the lightness of being, they prove that life without being ruthless is more advantageous. Then when these people are asked what their secret is, they may say that they do nothing other than organize their life according to the win-win principle (mutual benefit). In any case, they are no grouches, no pessimists or those who always feel sorry for themselves.

Even people who have catapulted themselves from bottom to top and who have become successful people have certainly also experienced setbacks. But what they did do is that after a step backwards they didn't resign and give up. They have not lost sight of their goal, namely the success of life. And because they took more steps forward than back, they ultimately achieved their goal.

The one who is successful is just starting there,
where the one who is unsuccessful ends his efforts.
Prof. Kurt Tepperwein

There are certainly past events that have had a negative impact on us. But there are also some that have shaped us positively. In a way, everyone has a history that has both negative and positive elements. But if we want to change our lives for the better - and we can if we are not mentally confused - we can do so by building on the positive. We try to leave the negative behind. The past is obviously over. And what is no longer there can have no influence. So how could the past influence us who we live in the present? First of all, what happened is over.

When we mentally take up past things, whether negative or positive, we bring them to life in the present. Only then they do have an impact on us. So, if we want the negative of the past not to have an impact on the present, we just let it rest. Instead, we can focus on the positive. **Do we have this possibility or not?**

Especially in training course for success, it is worked on recalling positive feelings from previous experiences in order to draw strength from it. They are feelings from experiences in which we either had a great success, where we might have had a winning streak, or which were just good for us. If we specifically recall negative feelings from past experiences, we will start the day with melancholy. We really have the choice at any moment to either gain strength or let our strength dissipate (wasted). It is our attitude alone that is crucial.

Even if I have experienced a major injury that cannot be healed, I am again faced with the choice from the time of the injury whether I simply accept the condition as given or whether I let me pull into the spiral of violence, self-pity or hate. We know that counter-violence against violence cannot reduce the violence, but rather intensifies it. If I let the spiral of violence turn, I stand in the fight and take an increased risk of being injured again. But I also have another choice. As I said, the other are imitators. The way I behave towards the other, the other behaves towards me, as a general rule. So how do I want the other behaving towards me?

If I can't or don't want to make friends with my counterpart, I can at least leave him alone, e.g. by doing no longer provoke. I can e.g. make it clear that I don't want to have a fight with him that I don't want to mess with him, that I don't want anything bad, and that I am peaceful. Then at least he might have a harder time being hostile to me.

Sometimes we have the impression that the chemistry is not right with the other and that it is therefore impossible to get along with him well. Is that really the case? Isn't everyone in a certain development and therefore doesn't everyone change his attitude towards the world over time? After all, everyone can change completely after drastic experiences, be t in the direction of the negative or the positive. I can also prove to the other person that I am different than he thinks I am. If I show him this, he must automatically change his mind about me. But if we are both too stubborn and proud to approach each other, nothing will change. Then we will convey to each other verbally or even only through body language that we don't want to have anything to do with each other. In particular, our body language reflects to the highest degree what attitude we have towards the other. If we want the other to respect us, we also have to respect him. And we can only do this if we change our attitude towards him. Otherwise we will use our body language (consciously or unconsciously) to convey to him that we are opponents of each other. If I signal my benevolence to the other person, he will also perceive this in some form.

Our body language can provoke and attack the other without verbal comments. And if we do not change our attitude towards him, we cannot expect the other to change his attitude towards us. Then we don't really give him a reason, right? Instead, the other feels confirmed and therefore sees no reason to behave differently than he has previously done. If the other person does not have the wisdom that working together and living for each other is useful for everyone involved, this does not mean that we should also act unwise. The wiser not only gives way, but shows strength through forgiveness, forbearance and compassion and also deserves respect. And who doesn't crave respect?

If I charge a certain person his past deeds every time, I project his behavior onto the present. Then this is like a target that releases energy so that this can be confirmed or repeated. If I then meet this person, I will get him to repeat his behavior by means of my attitude, be it in the form of my body language or by my behavior. Then I can assume with a high degree of probability that the other person can and does not want to do anything other than react as usual. To say that the other never can behave differently towards me as usual he does is without any evidence. Because if I don't take a step towards the other, I can't know if he would not even take a step towards me. Until I haven't done anything to find out, I cannot prove that the other cannot change.

The fact that we are different from one another is more proof that we can act differently. And if someone shows special behavior to me, it doesn't always have to do directly with me. It may well be that I remind the other of someone who has inflict on him something negative or something positive. This memory may have been triggered by a certain clothing, by a certain facial expression or by my special idiosyncrasy. This imprint initially puts me into a certain box by the other, whether with a good or bad label. The same can be the other way around. And I can only get out of this dilemma if I behave myself the way I want to behave myself the way from the inside out. Provided that I will be put in the special category 'courteous, kindly and the like' by the other there would no way in hell that I would try to get out of this category.

Whether I can change the other one or not should play a subordinate role. The main thing is that we act the way we want to give ourselves from the inside out. Otherwise we would be self-denying and would have a hard time looking into our own face. The worst would be if we would set ourselves to a level, that is unworthy of people, only because the other has low motives.

What is the use for us if we continue on an unforgiving path in the long run? A state of hatred, anger, disharmony and strife is grueling and self-destructive in the long run. Even if our paths diverge without internal reconciliation taking place, we will continue to carry this feeling in our hearts. Of course, our own body system is also a resonance-dissonance system that needs energy. We can certainly supply the body with energy through food, so that when you look roughly it shouldn't matter whether I'm in a bad or good mood. Is it really so? Our mood has a decisive influence on our body system. And this decides whether we let our strength fizzle out or whether we can use it in such a way that we can easily let regenerate our body.

If we feel tired and worn out, this is usually due to the fact that we are inhibited to swim in the stream of life - not to be confused with the stream of the mass -, that we constantly deny ourselves, that we are gotten involved with fighting and conflicting with others or/and that we go an unforgiving path. Only our attitude towards life is responsible for it. **We can change our attitude towards life.** If we change this, we will avoid the fight and do things that spur us on, but that do not inhibit us. Age does not matter. Age is not a real reason to make a change in our lives. Only the death of the body would prevent this change, provided there would be no life afterwards.

Often, when we find ourselves so little happy, we blame the evil world. There we missed many opportunities, which cannot be denied, to actively contribute to the increase in joy. So, is such a judgment about the world not too hasty or too clumsy? I think we only have the right to classify the world as bad when we have exhausted all the opportunities. Only when we have not achieved any noticeable improvement in our lives after these attempts and we are still standing without joy and without happiness, we do have the right to say that the world is bad.

With this consideration, however, it quickly becomes clear to us that this cannot happen. After all, such opportunities are certainly not exhausted when the world deteriorates. Because then the longing for peace and for a life for one another is all the greater. Especially in such a dark time like this, there are a lot of people who are longing for a friendly gesture or who want to hear something nice from the others. Why shouldn't we fulfill this wish if we can do it in a simple way anyway? In any case, nobody can say that he does not have the opportunity or the time to do this. **So, the world can never be so bad, so that no one can do something good.** Rather, it seems so that the condemnation of the world is a means of preventing to have to take our reins in our own hands.

Because we are always part of the world, any judgment about the world is always a judgment about ourselves. Instead of saying that the world is bad, we could say that the world needs me to get better. The possibility is there. It is waiting for us to grab the opportunity. If we did this, it got a little better. So, the judgment has to be put into perspective for the better. So, don't we have to say that the world is only as good or as bad as we want to believe it?

Even if someone else does something bad what I do for good, there is no reason to refrain from do loving things. Because whoever does not refrain from do loving things has no reason to reproach himself, he would not have at least tried it. Only those who have not tried to do something for good will be able to reproach themselves if they are not so dulled in spirit that they are not aware of that. And as long as there are people who are waiting for our kindness, our happiness is waiting for us. Because when we share our lives with each other, we have reasons to increase joy or, if it's difficult to be happy, to at least share suffering. Two or more of us can endure suffering much better than we can alone. Therefore, in our own interest, we are asked to lead the world for the better.

For that reason alone, to be able to endure the worst in the world, we have to connect with the other. A straw that stands lonely will buckle in the storm more likely than if it is surrounded by many straws. The straws of a grain field mutually offer wind protection. If we want to go our own way, we stand in this world like such a single straw. But if we go a way for being together and for each other, we are like part of a grain field. The storm cannot knock us down so quickly. Together we feel not only safer but also stronger.

If we want to have a better world, we ourselves are called upon to help make the world a better place, even if this is only in our small environment. It doesn't have to be the big thing. After all, none of us ask us to do something that we cannot do or that would let plunging us into a deep mental abyss of that we can no longer get out with ease. So, let's start in the next environment: at home, with the neighbor, at work, in school, on the street. It is enough if we do not want to do more than what is within our capabilities. In this way we create a better world in the active sense. And only in this way we can change the world to our advantage.

If you want to be happy, you have a duty to do something that makes you happy. The other can mean our luck. He constitutes our happiness if we approach him. Especially when someone is waiting to be able to share happiness with us, happiness is also waiting for us. Because no one can be happy alone (in isolation), everyone has the duty, if they want to be lucky, to seek and share their happiness with others. Nothing works without the other.

If you are not happy, you may pull others down, even if you don't want to do it. I do not want to assume that someone would not rather be happy than to be in the doldrums. Thus, if we cannot be happy, we have at least the duty to complain at least about our problems in such a way that the other can share it with us and that a solution to the problem is sought in the same way. At this point it should be said that we always need alternatives in terms of changes. The alternative must replace the previous situation. Otherwise there is a gap that is filled by the similar. For example, an unpleasant thought can be replaced by a loving thought in order to bring about a change in our state of mind towards the good.

What is empty needs to be filled.

We have to do something positive for hardship not to remain hardship. Hardship is not there to remain hardship or to be intensified. It is there to be diminished. So, we are always asked to actively contribute to the change. Our misery can hardly change on its own.

When the suffering is shared, it is half the size. Sharing suffering is not difficult. So, it isn't overcharging if we take care of the other's problem and share the suffering with him first. If, in the following, real solutions are tackled with the right means, the reduced suffering can even be transformed into joy.

Note. On the subject of 'sharing suffering' or 'compassion' it should be said that we have to be careful not to fall into the spiral of pity ourselves. This can happen when no one is looking for a way out. A way out or a solution should always be sought. And those who are not in pain or in conflict themselves can best help the other persons who are currently suffering if they express their compassion and if they look for solutions with them at the same time, provided the willingness is there. Otherwise, it is enough to just stick to our compassion, believing that the others can find their way out of the problem.

We cannot help others directly if it is a problem that is not directly related to us. Here we can only give advice on possible solutions. What the other person makes of it is his free decision. If the other person cannot do anything with our clues, this could partly be due to the fact that we ourselves cannot master life.

In any case, we can tackle problems that we have in common much better. These have to be solved primarily. We start with the immediate environment, i.e. in small things. If we have shown loyalty on a small scale, we can be loyal on a large scale. So, the exercise in the small is an exercise for the big. As long as we are not faithful on a small scale, we cannot be faithful on a large scale too. Only when we have managed to be faithful on a small scale we can be sure that we will not be too arrogant about the big one. Then we can also be sure that we will no longer fall. After all, it can always be said that pride comes before a fall. Seen in this way, we may even feel lucky if we are currently not dealing with the big one. As long as we are uncertain, the risk that something will not succeed is no different on a large scale than on a small scale. But there are enormous differences in the impact.

If problems seem big and very complex to us, they may just want to tell us that we are a little lower on the ladder of knowledge, but that never means that we cannot climb it up step by step. To do this, we have to tackle the problems step by step. There is little point in trying to solve them all at once. So why not start where it is easiest? Many small steps also result in a big step. Because a constant drop hollows the stone.

Now every situation offers the possibility of either finding a reason for increasing joy or, if we are not in the mood for joy, at least finding a reason for reducing suffering. Whoever searches shall find. In this case, we are doing something to keep peace. In peace, we can intuitively do the right thing in the right place at the right time, rather than in the strife.

We can also find a reason in every situation that brings anger, rage, hatred, quarrel, insult, injury, fear and isolation. The same applies here: *'Whoever searches shall find'*. However, we can be sure that we cannot solve the problem with this method, because instead we create new problems. In any case, we do something in this case that creates strife (discord, unrest). In strife or unrest, the risk of making mistakes is greater than in peace. Mistakes throw us back. We waste time that we lack elsewhere and have even less time than before. This is a vicious spiral that is building up.

Incidentally, it is not a great achievement if we always just wait for the other person to take the first step when it comes to getting closer to each other. Those who believe in themselves and want to take a responsible path do it the other way around. They take hold of their own reins and move ahead. Because they dare to get out of their own skin, they learn a lot more than when they hide from their problems. In the other case, if they only badmouth the others and don't give themselves a kick in making the first step to change, they don't learn and cannot become independent. Their area of responsibility is then limited to their own four walls. But our area of responsibility is limitless. After all, we influence the entire world with our thoughts and our actions.

> ***Who thinks he already knows everything***
> ***and unteachable holds onto his concept of self-crucifixion,***
> ***remains a child who steps on the spot.***
> ***Then how could he himself be a good advisor to others?***

Admitting one's own weakness is not hypocrisy. Those who admit it know that there is strength in them and that they have not yet been able to develop it. So, the likelihood is greater that they're striving for real strength. And because they then look at it as a target, they take steps towards it. Those who overplay weakness act as if they are strong. The more often they do this, the more likely they are believing to be strong. Then they deny their weakness. Anyone who denies it can't really look at his strengths. So, he does nothing to become strong.

Hardness has nothing to do with real strength. This shows the interplay of forces between hard and soft in nature. In the long run, the soft is stronger than the hard. In everyday life it looks as if we absolutely have to use the elbows, as if we have to fight and defend ourselves to be able to assert ourselves. We want to fight the hard with the same - that is, with the hard too. But it turns out again and again that these means lead to a vicious spiral that has no end.

Nature teaches us a different wisdom. **The soft water defeats the hard.** It 'defends itself' by clinging to the hard, embracing and encircling it. The water does not really hold itself back, because it is in confrontation with everything. If necessary, it can also be pushed back. But still it stays in touch and doesn't let up. As soon as the water comes to a gap, a crack or a fragile point, it gradually begins to clear its way there. It punctures the hard, makes it soluble, if necessary, so that it can be eroded and carried along by it.

The water collects wherever possible. It is infinitely patient in that regard. It can collect itself and wait until it turns into a raging river, in order to be able to carry everything away with it that stands in its way. It is also flexible here. Because what it can carry with it, it carries with it. The other thing that still stands in its way because it can still withstand a certain amount of resistance is worked on by the water until it can no longer withstand its pressure. Because the water is so flexible and so diverse, it can conquer the hard with an astonishingly minimal amount of energy. **The water stands in gentle but constant pressure in confrontation with the hard**.

When we work hard materials with hard materials, both materials deform over time, become soft, brittle or dull. They lose their original properties or wear off during their use. In order to get the original state back, they have to be worked up again with a relatively high expenditure of energy. Without processing, the hard material loses its function in the end. It becomes unusable.

Nature shows us how the soft overcomes the hard. We can use this phenomenon as a guide. We only have to understand this phenomenon correctly so that we can implement it in everyday life. Let's name a few keywords:

- Path of least resistance (this does not mean doing nothing and not throwing everything away because we are part of the flow of life).
- Maturity of time (thinking, saying or doing the right thing at the right place at the right time: sometimes silence is the order of the day, sometimes talking. Today it can be unfavorable with a certain truth, favorable tomorrow).
- Collection of external forces through connection (only together we are strong: try to bring the world to our side. Rather take a mediating or arbitrating position than being partisan).
- Collection of inner forces by finding inner peace (the strength lies in the silence).
- Being economical with energy (do not overexert yourself, pay attention to sufficient relaxation and appropriate regeneration phases of the body, do no double work, do not want to run up against a brick wall, sometimes hand over certain things).
- Proportionality (take correct means: figuratively speaking, do not cut butter with a chainsaw and do not want to saw a tree with a kitchen knife).
- Bring the means and path in line with the goal (optimal distribution of forces).
- Adaptation, flexibility, gentleness, persistence, patience.

The soft defeats the hard.

The hard and rigid are much closer to death than the soft. The maturing child, which still has soft bones, is flexible and capable of learning. A child can bow to external influences much more than an adult. It is more spontaneous, honest and more forgiving. Its anger is over much faster. If we get too angry and allow us to be overwhelmed by problems, we will be destroyed by the arising problems.

The adult who has come a little closer to death is stiffer, frailer and more stubborn. Older people generally find it more difficult to change their opinion than younger people. They are no longer so flexible, be it on the physical realm or in terms of adapting to constantly changing living conditions. The adults are not only much closer to physical death than the children, but have also lost a little more quality of life over the years. They lack a lot more vitality than is the case with children. Loss of quality with respect to life is something like an inner dying.

Older people are less likely to come up to others than children, which is why they generally lead a more isolated life than children. The children don't worry so much whether this or that contact is useful to them. The adults worry much more likely in this respect. This therefore prevents them from approaching the others. The more they distance themselves from others, the more they isolate themselves. Isolation is very closely linked to un-relatedness. And relationships without the involvement of the other are dead relationships. They pull us closer to death than to life.

Stubbornness, stiffness, rigidity, hardness, isolation and the like are fatal because they are against life. They are elements of a creeping suicide. Whoever opposes the flow of life and the course of things perishes and dies. Even in life, he's like a dead man.

Whoever works like a machine lives like a living corpse. Those life is dull, gray, loveless, listless, fearful, miserable and pitiful. Every day is almost like the other. If the day was gray yesterday, it is not much different today. On the contrary, the colors of everyday life fade more and more over time if we do not make life tasteful, loving, tender, gentle and soft. To do this, it is necessary to develop compassion for the world and for ourselves. Let us do ourselves the favor of having our stony heart enriched with love! It will do us good.

If you decide against life, you have to be afraid that you will at some point be of no use, because you are exhausted, frail, sick, stiff and inflexible. In the end, you are a part of the old guard because you will be no longer of any use. Instead, you will be a burden to others, which is why you can no longer stand yourself. You isolate yourself even more, which is why you approach death much more than life.

Man, when he comes into life is soft and weak,
and when he dies he's tough and strong.
The plants, when they come into life, are soft and tender,
and when they die they are skinny and rigid.
That is why the hard and strong are Journeymen of death,
the soft and weak Journeymen of life.

Lao Tzu (Tao te ching)

We have to learn to become soft like water. An adult, who is flexible, soft and gentle to himself as well as to those around him, lives his life in a way that is worth living. He can be like an adolescent into old age. His life is more full-filled, more peaceful, healthier and happier. Doesn't such a person get along with the world much better? And does he not know better about the mutual profit that life offers?

With each other instead of against each other.

It is in the nature of things that the other persons are more accommodating when they know that I share my life with them and that I want to be good with them. So, any attempt to involve the other persons in our life will involve in any case less energy expenditure than if we want to distance ourselves from them. Our experience shows that this is the case.

If e.g. we are quarreling with the other, we put a lot of energy into the situation, cause insult and injury, and yet make no step forward. We have only made a step forward when we have reconciled. But if we hadn't argued, offended and hurt, we could have come to the same result much faster and much easier. And whether all reconciliations really make everything forget is questionable. This always shows whether a certain deed of the past is charged from the other in one of the next conflicts.

Likewise, it is much easier to have a discussion if we get involved with someone and let the other have a say so that he can calmly present his position. Then he has the feeling of being taken seriously. He will also naturally come up with ideas that we can use for ourselves. He can also use our ideas in the same way. Mutual profit is greatest when we let others actively participate in our lives and when we treat each other peacefully and respectfully. This requires much less energy than through paternalism, know-all manner, arguments, anger and arrogance.

Even energy will be released if we get away from doing it all alone and instead do things for common goals. If we do and find things together, we have a reason to be happy. Joy can be contagious and build up. It gives us strength. This force is so great that it can also heal a part of the body. In addition, in this way the other person wants to stand less in our way because he knows that he also benefits from our actions. On the contrary, he lets us do more than before. In this way we can even extend our range of action.

Common goals are easier to achieve than individual goals.

After all, we have each other whether we want it or not. And because we have each other, it makes more sense to look for a way that not only benefits me but also the other. Because then how could he want to stand in my way? Isn't it even so that he wants to meet me if he knows that I want to beautify my and his life as well?

Everyone has their own special abilities that they can bring to the common cause. Not everyone needs to be able to do everything. What we cannot do, or can do only very badly, can be better and easier for others. What one does not have, the other has. So, it is only natural that we also involve the others and that their abilities do not have to be left unexploited. Things and people who are outside our own 4 walls must also be integrated. Life is a give and take. It has to be in flow.

In the cycle of nature, we can see the principle of give and take wonderfully well. What is taken from the earth is also given back to it. However, nature shows that not only one living being is involved in such a cycle. All earthly forms of being are involved in this. It seems that earthly life needs diversity in order to be preserved, because it cannot be denied that the preservation of life is based on the interaction of all forms of being. Every form of being has its special function or task within the earthly life.

Everyone also has a special function and/or task within people. Strictly speaking, we always have several functions and tasks that can change over time. According to our special functions and tasks, we contribute to the overall system. The better the interaction, the fewer problems are there. The worse the interaction are, the greater the problems.

Especially in a time of hectic and stress, it is not inappropriate to let go of things that are not within our ability to spend time on things that we can and want to do. What we are unable to do because it is not within the scope of our current capabilities is best left behind. So that's not how we do it! We can then use the time that is available to us to develop an ability or a quality that we consider desirable.

What can't I do and / or what I let best be? Here some examples:
- look into the future.
- read minds.
- know each other's motives exactly, even if they seem obvious to me.
- know what is good or bad for the other.
- be successful with my help when I take care of the needs of others and they have not asked me to help.
- know about things that I don't see.
- be successful in speculating about the lives of others.
- change the other without changing myself.
- change what is happened.
- prevent what comes anyway.
- understand the world in its entirety.
- understand at all without understanding with the heart.
- make no mistakes in the hectic or under pressure.

- can really maintain an opinion, especially one that no one wants to share with me.
- create peace in the other if he does nothing for his own peace.
- solve problems of others.
- solve problems alone.
- solve other people's conflicts without being conflict-free.

What can I do and/or what do I expand and develop?

- (can learn to) enjoy life.
- (can learn to) look at the good things in life: look for reasons that increase joy or reduce suffering.
- grab opportunities to actively contribute to the increase of joy.
- to love and appreciate the other person as to how he is or wants to be.
- give the other the feeling that he can master life or / and that despite his mistakes he is just ok.
- wish us and others good things.
- create inner peace.
- find peace of mind so that you can think, say or do the right thing in the right place at the right time.
- learn to listen.
- offer reconciliation after a dispute.
- allow myself and the other to confess my own mistakes, even if the other has also made mistakes without enumerating the other's mistakes.
- change myself (instead of wanting to change the other).
- develop skills or qualities that I consider desirable.
- push skills or qualities into the background that I don't want having in me.
- try to solve problems with that person with that I have these problems.

Solve problems together.

We cannot always understand situations we are confronted with. So, it makes little sense to want to understand them anyway. But what we can see is whether the situation changes over time for the better or for the worse. The change may go so slowly that we hardly notice it. But if we keep a diary, we can very well notice a change in ourselves. All we need to do is take a look at the past to see how insecure we felt at the time, what our problems were at the time, or what opinions we had back then. The many small changes that add up to a big change can be seen e.g. by looking back in the diary and comparing it with today. In any case, we can determine the direction in which t should go. So, it makes sense that we concentrate on changing life for the good and not for the bad.

Incidentally, no situation is identical to another. No situation really repeats itself. Only the behavioral patterns are repeated. This means that we always have to be prepared for something new. Seen in this way, we have to learn to cope with the situations again and again. There seems to be no end in sight to learning. **It is therefore not primarily a matter of learning to understand the situation as such, but rather of learning how we can change the situation in our favor - and this always means at the same time for the benefit of everyone.**

Because we have no problems without the other, it is also impossible to can solve problems without the other. If you want to solve problems without the other, you don't really solve them. What you do then is that you constantly create new problems. With the new problem the same question arises again: *'Did I try to connect with my problem partner or did i do something that distanced me from him?'*

As soon as one problem seems to be solved, the next one is approaching us. Today the problem is shown in green and tomorrow in blue. The problems have in common that the wrong attempt to solve them is associated with the increase in resistance, counter-actions, conflicts of interest and the like. The problems are growing. The legitimate attempt, on the other hand, lets the problems make smaller.

The easier way to solve problems is when I declare my problem and that of the other to be a common matter. This, because it is not wrong to say that your problem is my problem as well as my problem is your problem, although the weighting of a specific problem is slightly different for everyone. Just trying to make the other person know that my problem cannot be compared to any other prevents my problem from being solved. With this attempt we exclude us from the world around us. Then how could be solved my problem?

Achieve goals without conflict.

If we pursue a goal without involving the world around us, we can either not achieve the goal at all or only with a very high expenditure of energy. Furthermore, the goals are then limited to very few things that we cannot keep in the long run anyway. In the long run, this path is tiring, exhausting and ultimately unbearable.

If we align our goals so that they benefit not only us but also the other, we behave as it is appropriate to the principle of life. The resulting energy expenditure will then be minimized because the environment also accommodates our needs, especially as we are ultimately part of this environment. It is clear, if we pursue a common goal and involve others in the collection of ideas for the realization, that the likelihood of success is much greater than if we constantly are doing our own thing and ignore the others.

Given the large number of people and the many goals that exist, it is obvious that we should cause as few conflicts of interest as possible. I am not the only one who has needs, who has goals or who has the right to happiness, health and wealth. So why not to try to go a path of communality instead of a path of isolation? Even if there are no ideals that grant everyone equal rights and obligations, the striving for these ideals brings us more than if we do not take heed of them or even if we counteract them.

In any case, it is very clear that we are not going to reach a limit as quickly in trying to contribute to improving the world. This means that we can never get bored. Even if the world can reach the ideal state in which everything is found to be good, the boredom does not end. After all, the enthusiasm is so great that it doesn't want to go out. This can only go out when life as a whole expires. And whether this can be the case is likely to play a very subordinate role at the moment. This possibility could only play an important role when the universe approaches its death. Before this happens, however, we can say that if we want to participate in the improvement of the world, we have no disadvantage because we also benefit from it. The pursuit of personal well-being is more disadvantageous if it is put above the common good. But as long as we try to reconcile personal well-being with the common good, we cannot really lose. And there is no question that we will make it easier for us in the long run with this attempt.

The continuity paired with trust.

The question of our success in life always depends on how much we observe the law of energy minimization and how well we align our lives to it. If we pay attention to it, the main focus is already given. Falling backwards will then not really prevent us from taking steps forward again. After all, everyone has the freedom to choose a way of distancing themselves or a way of connecting. Nobody can make this decision for us. Neither can anyone prevent us from opting for one of the two ways if we don't allow it. And because of that, we have our lives in our own hands. We have our lives in our own hands both for good and for bad.

Every time we have failed to increase joy or reduce suffering, we have succumbed to temptation and opposed life. And because we opposed life, we also opposed ourselves, according to the law of actio = reactio. This is because we are part of life.

These are elementary life principles that are easy to understand. We only find it difficult to handle. Perhaps because there are so many who do it wrong. And because there are many who don't do it right, we believe there are no alternatives. In any case, there have always been people who have followed a path that has so to speak shown against the flow of the masse. There will always be such people in the future. And because there are such people, we have direct evidence that there is actually an alternative way to the ego trip. So, we also have proof that, despite being connected to everything, we can do something that enriches our life, that makes it more beautiful, and that makes us happier and more contented. We do not have to do anything that we cannot do or that we find difficult to do. Because if we observe the law of energy minimization, we are doing what is easiest anyway. And that we can achieve a greater deal in the long term by that than in the hectic, under stress and under pressure does not need to be mentioned specially.

We need each other to be happy. Strictly speaking, we don't need each other because we have each other. And because we have each other, we can achieve a greater deal with the other than without the other. So, it is obvious what we have to do to be happy.

When we are in an argument, we can remember to offer an alternative. We say to the dispute partner, for example: *'Let's not argue! Instead, let us consider together whether there is a solution that benefits everyone involved! '*. Every time we face someone and have a strange feeling with them, we can remember that we have each other after all. Then we can ask ourselves what it could be, that brings us closer together or that could be useful for both of us. We can always remember that we don't want to do anything that will put obstacles in our way.

Let us show our good intentions to the other, whether in words or simply by a small gesture of approach! Even if it is difficult for us to express our good intentions, we can do it in silence. We can imagine how our counterpart is dressed in light, how we smile at each other, how we approach each other or how we hug. There are no limits to the ideas. Every little gesture is a step in the right direction.

The power of positive intent.

Light is a symbol of love. If at the moment we cannot tell the other person that we love him, we can instead illuminate him with our light in our thoughts. This is a sign that we at least want to love or appreciate him. What I don't do well today,

I do better tomorrow. Or we just think: *'I want to love or appreciate you, even if I'm not able to do it so well at the moment. But I am willing to never stop trying until I succeed'*. We can briefly put our hand on the other's shoulder to let him understand that he is ok and that we are well disposed towards him.

We can ask the other how to deal with this or that situation now. What can we do differently, better or more sensibly? If we don't ask, we won't find out. Or, we can tell the other what we want. So, we can e.g. say: *'I would like to put forward my position on one thing or another'*. We could ask him if he has a little time for me to listen to me. This question is e.g. an open question because it gives the other person the choice to say yes or no. If we have questions for the others, it is never unwise to have open questions. Open questions are there to let the other person decide freely whether he wants to react to our needs or not without feeling bad about it.

We can also ask the other person how he feels, what he thinks or what he wants for us to do. Let us not be afraid of what it will be. Let us list by him as much as possible. Then we can e.g. say we would like to do this but would not like to do that. Let us say what we are daring to do or not to do, in which matter we stand behind it and in which not. There will always be something that will make everyone happy. It is important to find out. If we do this then we can be sure that life is much easier. We do the same the other way around, so that the other person knows how best to get involved.

A good and harmonious get-together could be a goal that we can tackle together. The more we know about each other, the more likely we are to find a consensus. Let's agree with the other what he wants to do! Let us look for common ground that are useful to everyone on the one hand and for which everyone can make their own contribution according to their individual abilities on the other hand.

We can start by doing certain things together consciously and try to enjoy being together. If e.g. we're lighting a candle when eating together it can increase the inner mood of everyone. There are many ways to make life more beautiful and loving. With this in mind, I wish you lots of fun and creativity.

2. Laws, rules and principles.

Summary.

a. All energetic processes follow the principle of energy minimalism.
b. Everything is related to everything else and is interrelated (example: nature, organism, family, state, etc.).
c. Everyone is part of the whole, which leads to the following because of our connectedness: 'What is good for the whole, is good for the individual and vice versa (example: nature, organism, family, state, etc.).
d. Laws or principles that can be derived from points a) to c):
   - Like in the small, so in the large and vice versa.
   - The win-win principle follows the principle of energy minimalism.
   - Since nature reconciles economy and ecology and is more effective than any man-made technology, creating the harmony of ecology and economy at the economic level leads to the highest possible effectiveness in productivity, at least in the long run.
e. Consequences for personal attitudes:
   - Everything I do, I always do for or against myself.
   - Nothing I do is not for or against myself at the same time.
   - We reap what we sow.

Example 1: If I am benevolent towards everything, I radiate this benevolence. The other feels this in some form and can hardly do anything other than being benevolent towards me too (-> good prerequisite for mutual profit).

Example 2: Conversely, when I'm grumpy and negative, the other feels it in some way. That then can hardly do anything other than distance himself from me or isolate himself from me. Then he will be reluctant to do anything for me (-> bad condition for mutual profit).

<u>Here are the individual principles, rules and laws in detail:</u>

The principle of similarity (transfer from the small to the large). The analysis of our teaching unit is not difficult, although life may seem very complex. We can divide the world, so to speak, into units (quanta), for which the principle of similarity applies. What applies on a small scale also applies on a large scale; and vice versa. The principle of similarity is ultimately based on the hermetic analogy law 'like above, so below'. The body is, so to speak, a micro-universe consisting of parts that exist in a hierarchical order but also in symbiosis with each other. But the body as a micro-universe is not a closed universe, but is part of an even larger unity. One of these units is humanity, which is also hierarchically structured. We find hierarchical structures in families, groups, companies, states and other groups. Furthermore, together with minerals, plants and animals, mankind forms earthly life. This is a unit that is also well structured and whose parts also exist in symbiosis with one another. The earth, which carries earthly life, is also embedded in the cosmic structure of the universe. Then the material levels form units that are subordinate to the spiritual levels. And so, there is a hierarchical structure within the universe, which itself, as we shall see in Volume 2, is embedded in a hierarchical structure.

So, it is obvious that not a single unit system is self-contained because there are overarching things everywhere, which in turn affect and influence other unit systems. The mutual influence may lead us to believe that these systems are very complicated and therefore very difficult to get to grips with. This is a fallacy, because the law of analogy teaches us otherwise. Because of the similarity principle, it is sufficient to pick out a few unit systems as an example to give us an idea of the spiritual laws. This facilitates our analysis and also reveals that the fundamental principles of life are very simple. The external things may seem very complex, but they are not at all complicated.

Every unit system stands and falls with its inner structure. If a state system has the structure of a house of cards, the best strategy is of no use in stabilizing the state system. A state structure must be structured in such a way that it is clear and reliable both from top to bottom and from bottom to top. It is no different with the functioning of a living organism. All cells and all organs have to work hand in hand so that the organism is functional in the long run. The organism must be able to give every part everything it needs, just as the part must give the organism everything it needs. If the organism as a whole is doing well, every single part of the organism is doing well too.

Energy minimalism (imitating nature). If we closely observe nature, we see that it works far more effectively than any technology made by humans. The minimalism of nature is based on the fact that, despite the diversity each of its parts works hand in hand according to its systems and functions. Each of its parts has a specific task that is conducive to the whole. It is like an organism, of which the parts (cells, organs, limbs) also work hand in hand in accordance with their systems and functions. Although nature is wasteful, the interaction of its parts allows for minimalism in terms of energy and maximalism in terms of effectiveness. This effectiveness can also be applied to people's daily life.

When we team up with each other and share certain tasks, life is easier, whether in the private or business sphere. If each individual cooks their own soup, far more energy and time is required than if, for example one shops and washes up and the other cooks. Or a company that has to stand up to strong competition can no longer afford not to place teamwork at the top of the list these days. Not everyone does the same thing, everyone does something different, if possible according to their ability. The better the individual can put his skills into play and the better it is worked hand in hand, the more harmonious the interaction, the easier the work and the more effective the company's productivity. *In any case, we can give countless examples to make it clear that a life of being together and for each other is an easier life than a life of ego trip, of individual efforts or a life against each other.*

Whoever goes a way of conflict, of ego trip, of fighting and the like, violates the law of energy minimization and goes against life. The result is struggle, exertion and fatigue. On the other hand, a life with each other and for each other fulfill the law of energy minimization. In such a life, such strong forces can be released that we hardly have the feeling of exhaustion and weariness. At the end of the day, we may sometimes be tired. But this will be combined with such a good feeling that we will be back full of energy the next day. We are much more likely to create conditions that allow body and mind to regenerate. If we instead face a fight the next day, we will not even be able to muster half of this strength by comparison. Then we would likely prefer to hole up and stay home alone. There we would be in the doldrums and isolate ourselves even more from life.

Practical example of an energy minimalism: strive for common goals. Common goals are easier to achieve than single goals (Explanation see above).

Personality and identity (development capacity in the collective): Anyone who believes that they lose their identity in the collective is extremely wrong. On the contrary, whoever wants to disconnect from it is lonely and abandoned. **This fact is easy to understand when we consider moments in which we are cut off from the outside world.** We feel lonely and abandoned. We feel life dreary, sad and lifeless and feel closer to death than life. At such moments, we don't even have the ability to recognize ourselves because we can't classify. We do not know who we are or where we belong.

There is a lack of comparison with the diversity that life as a whole offers us. Furthermore, we only show very few of the many qualities that are within us. And, the longer such a lonely state persists, the more we limit ourselves to the few qualities that we consider appropriate n such moments. The other properties are left unexploited, wither and are forgotten. Therefore, we can no longer believe that completely different things are in us. Because also the hidden (not unfolded) properties belong to us and have something to do with our identity.

With the decoupling from the collective, which furthermore is only partially possible, there is a loss of identity. The greater the decoupling or isolation, the more we lose our own identity. The isolation makes us lonely. In loneliness we get into personality states that literally put us in lethargy. This lethargy prevents us from being able to develop freely. But freedom is an important aspect that is part of our identity. So how could isolation have anything to do with our identity?

If we focus our lives on doing something that we can share with the collective, we will experience completely different things. We will arouse enthusiasm, happiness and belonging. Powers are released. These can become so strong that almost nothing is too much for us. We will even be amazed at what we can do. In loneliness, on the other hand, almost everything is overcharging us.

The current power of everyone is always based on how they see themselves in relation to the collective and how they want to involve themselves. The collective lives through each individual. The more individuals work hand in hand, the better it is for the collective and thus also for its members. The best way to keep the collective is when all of its members fully support the idea of the collective. Then the collective too can fully support each of its individual member.

Transfer to a company. A company is a community that has a certain idea that it markets in some form. It does not matter whether this idea relates to a service or to the production of a certain product. Every employee is part of this company and in the best case fully supports the idea of this company. The optimal prerequisite for this is when each employee can feel part of his company and when he can optimally contribute to it according to his gifts, abilities or talents.

Now there are various tasks that not every employee can perform. What one can do well, the other one can do less well. But the latter can do something other better. In this respect, care should be taken to ensure that each employee can contribute in a way that best suits his skills and that he is quite devoted in his task. This also means that every employee is given a certain amount of freedom that allows them to develop.

This does not mean that the company should not set basic requirements. This is necessary to create an orderly framework. But within this framework, which should be clearly worked out, the area of freedom for every employee should be guaranteed.

If the employees work hand in hand according to their skills, it is optimal for the company. Not only that, then all parts of this company benefit (win-win principle) too. If every employee is enthusiastic about the idea of a company, it doesn't really matter who the idea came from.

The motto of a modern company that could be pursued could be that the employer-employee relationships must address the win-win-principle. The challenge of a company is, of course, how it can create optimal framework conditions so that everyone can contribute optimally to the idea and that everyone can feel part of the company.

Possibilities:
- The company boss should not shy away from the relationship with his employees, who are virtually at the bottom of the task hierarchy, and should take care of their problems when they appear (employee meetings).
- Certain reprimands should make sense if someone moves out of the frame and endangers the win-win principle.
- The company philosophy should be worked out right from the start and it should be clearly stated that every employee is valuable and that no arrogance is tolerated.

Imitate the action of the water. The water is soft, smooth and holds itself back when the path is blocked. **The softness stands for gentleness.** So, let us be gentle towards the world around us! The water seeks the way through cracks, channels, holes and don't let prevent from taking detours. The constant dripping, however small it may appear, can wear away the stone. So, the soft water defeats the hard; not immediately, but steadily. **The steadily dripping stands for patient perseverance, in which we constantly believe in our strength and persistently build on every step, no matter how small.** So, let us be patient and let's wait until we can take full action! The water collects until it can step over the banks or over other obstacles. Then it can become a torrent and sweep away everything that stands in its way. Now the path of the water is straighter, clearer and more powerful. If the raging torrent decreases, the water can also take detours again. It takes exactly the way that is the most advantageous for it. **So, let's gather our strength until we can use it effectively!** Once our strength has evaporated because we have not ensured that it can flow in as good as we have used it, it is necessary to collect ourselves again. **So, just as water follows the path of least resistance, we should also strive for the path that obeys the law of energy minimization.**

The Pareto principle (a peculiar disproportion). A company has a certain number of sales representatives in the external sales who ensure the turnover of the company. It can be seen that regardless of the company and the product, 20% (**80%**) of the sellers generate 80% (**20%**) of sales. Likewise, in all sales sectors 20% (**80%**) of the salespeople have a success rate of 80% (**20%**) in relation to their offers.

This ratio is commonly known as the Pareto principle, named after Vilfredo Pareto (1848-1923), who had found this relationship in many other areas of life. Surely it can be argued whether the numbers still match so exactly everywhere today or not. **However, the phenomenon of the strong imbalance is undeniable.** And now it should be about it.

Sellers in sales psychology know a similar relationship. For example, 80% of the customer's purchase decision is made from the subconscious. It has to be said that our subconscious can interpret the non-verbal body language of the other very well, whereby this body language provides the other with additional information. According to this, what we speak with the mouth should only contain about 20% of all information that we convey to the other through our body.

A lot of people believe that they are often better off in this world using any kind of deception than acting in an honest manner. Therefore, they are not infrequently tempted to fool the other which does not correspond to their innermost attitude. **And exactly this discrepancy is reflected in the entire body language, which is reflected in the success of life.** If e.g. conscious perceptions and unconscious messages do not match, our conversation partner behaves about 80% according to their unconsciously received messages. Accordingly, the seller will struggle to cover up an internal discrepancy and to persuade the potential buyer to buy.

Body language is a reflection, of what it looks like inside of us. It almost reflects our state of mind. Body gesture and state of mind represent an inseparable system of unity. Because of this, the state of mind can hardly be occulted by body language, unless we are appropriately trained. But those who are well trained in this regard will also have gotten to know themselves better, which is why at least they strive in part for a harmonious balance between their mental attitude and their body gestures.

The further we are away from our inner harmory, the greater is the discrepancy between body language and our personal behavior, the more we are in discrepancy with the world around us. **This discrepancy manifests itself in the fact that our life's success leaves something to be desired.** In order to make this discrepancy clearer to us, the following theses are presented.

Theses on the Pareto principle.
a. With regard to our objectives, 80% of the time we deal with things that only make up 20% of life's success.
b. We are looking for salvation success 80% in medication or in material application and 20% in our thoughts or in our own behavior.
c. In 80% of people, the life-success rate is only 20% if success is that what really fills us, i.e. if job and vocation match.
d. We are 80% dominated by a thinking system that turns spiritual laws upside down (this thinking system, for example, does not take into account that the soft defeats the hard, that pressure always creates counter-pressure, that pride always comes before the fall and that in the hectic and stress we always make mistakes that we have to iron out again, which often takes more time than if we take the time to act calmly and deliberately, for which reason we can't really gain time).
e. People in the civilized world consume around 20% healthy food and around 80% 'damning' or not really healthy food. In order for the body to remain reasonably healthy and vital, the relationship would have to be turned around.
f. Around 80% of human food is cooked, fried and / or baked, while the raw vegetable diet only makes up around 20%. This manifests itself among other things by the fact that 90% of the people in the civilized world have an acidified body.

g.   We humans unconsciously waste 80% of our time on things or topics that do not really help us to develop. What we achieve during this time 'harms' us more than it helps us. The remaining 20% of the time we take for ourselves and our fellow human beings is not enough to compensate for the bad state of affairs.

Although the numbers in the relevant areas or topics are not necessarily accurate, they should at least us show the dis-proportionality that we can change. **At this point it should be noted that the Pareto principle is not really a law, after all there are exceptions to all related topics or things.** The Pareto principle is therefore a rule that is known to have exceptions. This in turn means that we can make the rule an exception and the exception a rule. So, if 80% of our efforts had previously only led to 20% success, by means of a suitable change of behavior and re-thinking about things we may now need to spend only 20% of our efforts to an 80% success.

From the Pareto principle we can see in general where the current behavior of people in dealing with themselves, with others and with nature has led. This behavior has led to bad state of affairs crying out for a turnaround. It is the turn *away from the elbow behavior, away from the rivalry thinking, away from a life against each other* **towards a meaningful life, which is based on a win-win principle, on a life of togetherness and on a life for one another**.

The golden rule. This easy-to-understand rule states: "'What you want people not to do to you, don't do it to anyone else". Whoever pays attention to this and tries to act according to it in a practical sense, develops more and more a feeling of mindfulness as well as of togetherness.

3. The teachings of life are (Keyword-like):

- that we always lose with hardness (the soft defeats the hard).
- that pride always comes before the fall.
- that pressure, tension and violence are always associated with counter pressure, counter tension and counter violence.
- that in the hustle and bustle and stress we always make mistakes that we have to iron out, so that we cannot really save time with them.
- that nobody can flee from their learning tasks; as long as we want to do this, these tasks keep catching up with us.

4. Tips for observing the law of energy minimization.

Problems are, so to speak, hurdles or resistances that have to be overcome. There is the term 'whole heap of problems'. From this perspective, we constantly climb mountains when we tackle problems. Some mountains are more difficult to climb than others. And that is exactly why we have to learn to set priorities in our lives.

As soon as we turn a problem into a problem, it grows. We literally slip into the problem. It embraces, clasps and engulfs us. This does not solve the problem. Problems can only be solved if we face the problems. So, we are not going into the heap of problems, we climb it.

The mountain is, in a sense, an obstacle that is not always to be avoided, but sometimes to be overcome. Some obstacles can actually be skipped. Others, like the mountain, have to be climbed step by step. Once at the top of the mountain, a wonderful sight awaits us. The mountain peak is a place that enables us to grasp (overlook) everything. It enables greater insight. The symbolic mountain climb has a sense. It can be an overarching goal.

Some people who want to be inspired climb a mountain. They meditate up there to get into a state of consciousness that brings them closer to God or the Higher Self. The mountain is therefore symbolic in several ways. In order to be able to climb the mountain, the forces must be available. Let us consider two attitudes towards climbing a mountain.

Attitude A.

- I have no desire to struggle with that.
- I could do something other than mountaineering.
- I don't know what to do up there.
- that is not good for me because I can injure myself on the way.

Attitude B.

- the mountain is a challenge.
- the climb gives me the feeling that I have mastered something.
- I enjoy the panorama.
- if I conquer this mountain, I conquer an even more difficult mountain.

When two people, who have roughly the same physical constitution (condition), climb a mountain, the ascent of the mountain is felt differently depending on the attitude. Those with posture A will find it harder to climb mountains; the others easier.

Understanding what is good or useful is very important. This applies analogously to all problem solving. If we want to deal with problems, the best way to do it is to tackle this problem with full force to solve it. So, don't jump into the problem with full force, but jump over the hurdle with full force or climb the problem heap. At this point I would like to remind you of the softness and flexibility of the water. We don't want to force anything, but we also don't want to run away. The best way to tackle the problem is to keep in touch and overcome (solve) the problem with gentle but constant force. If we do not recognize the meaning of the problems, it is always difficult for us to deal with them.

Now there are many situations in our life that we have to master. So, we always face several problems that we always have to solve with the world around us. We may not know where to start. It is therefore important to set priorities. What is easier for us has priority. When it comes to spontaneous actions, we shouldn't think too much about whether it's good or not. Ultimately, these come from an inner impulse. And we shouldn't usually suppress this.

Nevertheless, there are also situations that really push us to take a certain action, even though we know that we will find it difficult to do so. We can feel an urge to do something because we feel pressured, because there is a compulsion, or for other uncomfortable reasons. In any case, there is also the risk that lets knock our heads against a brick wall, so to speak. So that we don't get on the wrong track, it is helpful to pay attention to the signs that accompany us during this project (plan). In order to understand this better, we again consider the two mountaineers, one of whom is in posture A and the other in posture B.

Assume that the two climbers are friends. The one who really wants to climb the mountain tries to convince his friend to come along. But the friend has no real desire and also has many reservations. He may think that instead he could do something else that would bring him more. On the other hand, he doesn't want to disappoint his friend. So, he may fall between two stools because he doesn't know what to do now. A lot can happen in the meantime, especially if the mountain climb is still distant in time.

In any case, the likelihood is not small that the one who actually do not want to climb the mountain is more likely to get sick or injure himself in the meantime. If he defends himself internally, he may subconsciously ensure that he hasn't to climb the mountain. He lets subconsciously something happen that prevents him from mountaineering, such as: he injures himself or gets sick or he invents a white lie. But if he had let his friend know from the start that he did not want to climb the mountain with him for this or that reason, he could have avoided a lot of inconveniences. He shouldn't have fooled himself or his friend. In addition, he was unable to convince himself whether his friend was a real friend. After all, one can expect a friend not to cancel the friendship because of a no, unless it is directed against him.

Even when the climbing of the mountain takes place, it can happen that the friend with posture A gets injured on the way to the summit, that he gets blisters on his feet or that other unpleasant things come up to him. In any case, it will be things that make it clear to that with attitude A or maybe to both that climbing the mountain is not his thing. The one with attitude A has denied himself because he was dishonest not only to his friend but also to himself. In addition, he has not found out whether his friend is a real friend. In addition, he has failed to do something else that would have served him better. Instead, he possibly had experienced something that was bitter for him and maybe for his friend too.

The side effects of such a venture are nevertheless signs that can be interpreted. We can recognize from them whether a thing is worthwhile or not. In particular when unpleasant things occur, the project has to be reconsidered. In any case, then it will take a lot of strength to complete the project anyway. And whether we won anything by this is questionable.

It can be said that activities in our lives are most fruitful if the law of energy minimization is not violated. Of course, it is not always easy to see which path involves the least resistance. But there is a rule of thumb here: **If your devotion to a particular project is small and the resistance is high, it is better to choose another option of action and to do other things instead.** We may feel compelled to do these things out of constraints, fears or other motives. But in every situation, there will always be the question of whether there is another way, another means or even another goal for which we can choose instead.

The devotion is small if e.g. the enthusiasm is low, there is no great desire, our hearts were not entirely in it or we do not promise much from the project. The resistance can take many forms as follows:
- the project does not work or works only with great difficulty
- the means are not the right means (disproportionate)
- we make many mistakes
- the dangerous situations are increasing
- accidents and damages occur
- the body opposes (headache = we're racking our brains over a problem), body hurts or gets sick (tends to hinder us in doing something)

- The other shows his reluctance or makes counter-suggestions or admonishes us.

Especially when there's a lot of resistance and things don't work the way we want it, they are a warning sign to us. The warning sign wants to point out another problem solving or other things that can or should be done instead. But if we are overflowing with energy and despite the resistance, this project is still a challenge for us, we should keep up the course. Then the dedication is great. The undertaking will definitely have been worth it. Even if the project did not work, at least we have had enough experience to recognize that this method is not the right one. Finally, knowing that something is not going to help us we will not try again it in this way. We can check this method off and free ourselves for new things and ideas. So, if we learn from mistakes, we have saved energy and time in the long term too.

5. Conclusions from Chapter I.

Life teaches us that the best way to act is to take the path of togetherness and for one another. We don't need to believe in God. And the question of whether our life continues after the death of the body does not change this fact. If it continues after the death of the body and if we are immortal spirit, the path leads at the end with a high probability to God. Ultimately, sooner or later experience leads everyone to realize that the path of togetherness and for one another is the best path ever.

Why doesn't everyone have this knowledge? If you look at the world superficially and don't really get to the bottom of it, you run the risk of coming to results that incorrectly reflect the regularities of the world affairs. And because there may be many who look at the world superficially, the impression can be given that the many are in the right position.

If people walk over dead bodies or otherwise cheat through life and thereby give the impression that they would have won a happier lot, this is a deceptive impression. Because whoever does something that hurts or exploits others cannot live without guilt. And a feeling of guilt is not exactly a good feeling of life, even if it may look different superficially. If people seem to be doing well superficially, it can look very different inside. But because we don't see the inside and instead look at the outside, we get possibly a wrong picture. And a wrong picture leads us to wrong conclusions.

Regardless of where we are in the development or what ailments we have, we always have two choices. Either we isolate ourselves even more from our fellow world or we connect with it. The connection makes us happier, while the isolation makes us even unhappier.

A person who is so strong in the mental entanglement that he is paralyzed and therefore currently has no possibility to choose between the two paths will not feel addressed here. But this is no proof that a way of living together and for each other is no better than a way of isolation. Because someone who has no choice will never have cast an eye on this or that way. So, the question doesn't necessarily arise for him. And yet the question is open whether such a person doesn't also have this choice, even if it is only in a subtle (hardly noticeable) way. After all, why shouldn't a person in great need of help, if he is lovingly cared for by others, feel that it is good not to be alone? Likewise, the question is open if for a mentally paralyzed person there was the opportunity after all to free himself from his mental paralysis if it continues life after the death of the body.

II. The influence of Spirit on matter.

1. Experiments and other evidence.

In this chapter, well-known experiments are listed which indicate that spirit can influence matter. The experiments or experimental set-ups that establish the influence of spirit on matter are among other things as follows:

* Robot Chick Experiment, where a chick is shown to induce a robot to be near it, even though the robot is programmed so that its paths are random: https://www.youtube.com/watch?v=M0cURvVvBew

* Epigenetics: 'The mind is stronger than the genes', Bruce Lipton: https://www.youtube.com/watch?v=HLJWj_hNki4

* Epigenetics, water and rice experiments by Masaru Emoto, placebo-nocebo effect: https://www.youtube.com/watch?v=livLliVWWoY

* Plant experiment: Dr. Ing. Cleve Backster: https://dieter-broers.de/unsere-gedanken-sind-nicht-in-unserem-kopf-begrenzt/

* Carpenter Effect (Phenomenon that seeing a certain movement and - to a lesser extent - thinking about a certain movement triggers the tendency to perform this movement): https://www.hypnoseausbildung-seminar.de/hypnoseinfo/hypnoselexikon/carpenter-effekt.html

* Evidence that consciousness and the physical world are interdependent: https://transinformation.net/wissenschaftliche-studien-die-beweisen-dass-bewusstsein-und-die-physische-welt-einander-beeinflussen/

* PEAR - PSI Research at Princeton University, Influence of Mind on Machines: https://vimeo.com/4359545

* **The Experiments of Dr. William A. Tiller.** Dr. Tiller, Professor Emeritus in material science and engineering at Stanford University, has studied

mind over matter phenomena. His experiments have shown that humans are able to raise or lower the pH-value of water voluntarily (mentally). The pH increased or dropped according to these intentions at an amount of up to 1.5. The odds are, by chance, a million to one.

* **The double slit experiment revisited.** Dean Radin is chief scientist at the IONS (Institute of Noetic Science, founded by astronaut Edgar Mitchell), and a member of the adjunct faculty in the Department of Psychology at Sonoma State University. He re-examined the double slit experiment, in order to proof the possibility of the power of spirit over matter. Radin set up the equipment provided for this in a room shielded from electromagnetic signals and physical vibrations. The trial persons imagined that they put their mind inside the box and were watching the photons go through the slits. It could be shown, that the trial persons were able to cause a significant shift from the expected wave pattern. So, many particles were observed when there should only have been waves recorded. It was significant that experienced meditators were better able to cause the shift than the non-meditators.

* **The Experiments of Intention:** With a sensitive enough camera it is to observe, that all living things emit so called bio-photons. Dr. Gary Schwartz from the University of Arizona ran an experiment which shows, that the leaf of a plant that received people's intention glowed far brighter than the leaf that did not receive intention. This experiment was successfully repeated many times. <u>Another experiment:</u> A large number of people in Australia sent energy to seeds of a plant. The charged seeds did indeed grow faster. In one of these experiments, the charged seeds grew twice as tall as the seeds of the control group. Such or similar experiments have been repeated with many large groups around the world, all demonstrating the power of mind (spirit) over matter.

* **The Global Consciousness Project.** The Global Consciousness Project, which has been running for almost 20 years, examines the impact of people's thoughts and feelings around the world when they think and feel the same things. There are currently Random Number Generators (RNGs)

in 70 locations around the world that create sequences of unpredictable ones and zeroes. When major events occur, like 9/11 or the death of Princess Diana, the numbers stop appearing so random. At these highly eventful and emotional times, the numbers line up amazingly well, breaking the odds of a trillion to one against the null hypothesis.

* **Mental training to increase performance.** It is well known that mental training in competitive sports is gaining in importance, because of improving performance in sports. People can also let grow their muscles by means of the power of thought:
  https://www.newscientist.com/article/dn1591-mental-gymnastics-increase-bicep-strength/,
  https://www.ncbi.nlm.nih.gov/pmc/articles/PMC3783980/

It is not necessarily the case that we have to point out the miracles of Jesus in order to testify to the power of the Spirit. More and more people testify that they have spiritual powers that cannot be explained with the help of material laws. Examples for this are:

Body control. Especially talented people, such as Yogis are able to achieve a targeted regulation of the organs such as heartbeat or regulation of the body temperature.

Physiological changes under hypnosis. What yogis can do, normal people can do if they can go under hypnosis. Under hypnosis, we are able to lower or increase muscle tension, heart rate, blood pressure and / or stress hormone levels.

Abilities in spontaneous actions. At times when we don't ponder, we can lift a car with our bare hands to free someone underneath. These and other things are reported in the world from time to time.

Spontaneous healings. It also happens from time to time that people e.g. undergo spontaneous healing after a death sentence.

Walk over red-hot coals. In 2001, 22 people between the ages of 7 and 80 set a Guinness record by safely crossing a carpet of ember of 111 meters. According to reports, this world record was improved to 222 meters on March 13, 2003 in La Balmondière, near Mâcon in France. The 16 participants were said not to have sustained any major injuries. On March 22, 2003 in St. Lorenzen (Austria) the world record in this discipline was improved to 250 meters. Now you can ask yourself whether without good mental preparation we are able to do something like this at all?

Take an ice bath for a long time. Wim Hof, a Dutch extreme athlete, was able to stand up to his neck in ice water for an hour, 52 minutes and 42 seconds. He is also able to do other incredible things:
https://de.wikipedia.org/wiki/Wim_Hof

The daily and budget plans. Even the daily planning and budget planning are a bit of attempts to live out our creative nature. The principle is to imagine the result or write it down as you want it to be. You act as if it has already happened. Then you align your life or activities towards this result until you have achieved it.

The power of thought has been highlighted in sales and management training for years. The power of thought is also the main theme of the film 'the secret', in which scientists from various disciplines have their say. This clearly shows that we are the creators of our situations. Perhaps an indication of a book in which the scientific evidence for the self-healing powers is provided:
https://www.amazon.de/Mind-over-Medicine-Wissenschaftliche-Selbstheilungskraft/dp/3466345979

All these mentioned experiences let observe the influence of mind on matter. Starting from the fact that more and more experiments prove the influence of the spirit on matter, we have a first assumption/statement about what life is. **Life is able to influence purposefully or consciously: 1st basic principle of life**. The aforementioned studies show e.g. the influence and effect of human mind on water, food, plant growth and other things and how the animal mind (chicken) influences robots.

Nevertheless, the <u>mind</u> is only a small aspect of <u>Spirit</u>, who we will get to know better in the following study. Here it will be shown the difference between the mind and Spirit. While the mind can only direct material things or energy in a limited way, the Spirit is capable to cause, maintain, direct, control and resolve matter in an unlimited way. Mind without the higher aspects of Spirit is not capable to cause (manifest) or resolve matter.

2. Conclusions from Chapter II.

Although the immaterial spirit cannot be determined directly, his influence on matter can be demonstrated. More and more experiments and studies show the influence of the spirit in humans and animals on water, food, plant growth, machines and other things.

III. Our spiritual origin and what this means for us.

Note: This section shows what our true independence is based on.

We live in a time when more and more people question things and no longer want to blindly believe those responsible (politicians, doctors, teachers, ...). But it is also a time when more and more people are resigning or giving up. They know that things cannot really go on as before, but they don't know how this could be done. The doctors are 'married' to the pharmaceutical industry, the politicians are under pressure from the lobby associations, and the journalists report what one should hear or read without becoming neutral. Then we also hear about a certain elite who wants to take over the world and whose force is supposed to influence the system in such a way that all those who support this system work towards this elite. If you don't play along, you lose your job or are defamed or in some way pushed into a corner. It seems to be a vicious circle that cannot be broken. One can almost only resign, be frustrated and express justified worries and fears. Even the belief in God doesn't seem to help much. Is it really like that? Is there no alternative?

To answer this question, we cannot avoid addressing the deeper causes of the world problem, the energetic hierarchies as well the source of power.

1. The hierarchies (puppet player).

In the meantime, physics has come to the realization that there is not only matter alone. In doing so, it comes to the conclusions that matter only has a 4% share in the universe. The rest of it consists of dark matter and dark energy. Here are the proportions as postulated by physics:
- **Matter: ca. 4% (directly detectable)**
- **Dark matter: ca. 23 % (indirectly detectable)**
- **Dark energy: ca. 73 % (indirectly detectable)**

Dark matter and dark energy are physically not directly visible. But their influences can be determined through observation. And when physics demands that dark matter and dark energy exist due to observation, it ultimately confirms what the spiritual sciences have long said. They say that man has not just a physical body, but also has higher, subtle bodies. In relation to our world system, this means that it can be roughly divided into two parts: this world (visible) and the hereafter (invisible).

The two parts of the world can be divided further, whereby we can divide them into several floors (levels) like the floors of a building, to call a metaphor. In this metaphor, however, these levels have no spatial arrangement but a purely energetic arrangement. We can take a mental picture as follows: Our material building blocks consist largely of protons and neutrons. The material world thus consists of proton and neutron vibrations. For their part, neutrons and protons are undershoots of higher-vibrating quarks.

The quarks together result in the level of the quark oscillation, whereby we have only changed the magnifying glass here and not the place of observation. Depending on the magnifying glass (on energy), we see either protons/ neutrons or quarks at the same point in space-time.

If we could also examine the quarks in more detail, we would probably find that the quarks also are densifications of even higher energy vibrations, which we can call ether vibrations. Similarly, the ether vibrations would be more fundamental than the quark vibrations. We would see the ether vibrations if we made the magnifying glass on the quarks even bigger (even higher energy); and again, in the same place. It is currently not possible for physicists to generate such high energies in their elementary particle accelerators in order to demonstrate the ether vibrations. Likewise, the vibrations of the ether have so far not been registered directly by any technical devices. **But such and even higher energetic vibrational levels can be perceived by particularly gifted people.**

There are many indications that our universe presumably has higher vibration levels. For example, we know terms such as "upper world" or "lower world(s)" in religious writings and / or fairy tales as well as the statement that God is understood as our basis of life. God could therefore be seen as the highest state of being of the highest vibration level. Last but not least, this idea can be harmonized very well with the Brane models of physics, according to which the vibrational level of matter is located on the outermost shell of the 5-dimensional sphere (bubble). The universe as a whole would represent this 5-dimensional sphere (bubble), which is filled with energy in the innermost.

The other levels, we can imagine as spherical shells, which are placed within the outermost spherical shell, in which the physical layer is the outermost spherical shell. The more you go into the inside of the sphere, the higher would be the energy of the corresponding levels. This means, that the dimension, which is directed towards the centre of the sphere, is no spatiotemporal dimension, but a kind of frequency dimension or spiritual dimension.

The further we go mentally into the inside of the sphere, the more spiritual we get or the higher energies (frequencies) we're dealing with. Inwards, the energy levels are getting more and more similar to pure vibrations. Entirely in the interior, the Spirit will be completely pure energy vibration (without any compaction). That means, that the energy there would be pure light.

By the selective selection of energy generation (in physics) and/or by the selective resonating of our spirit to a certain level of vibration, we can filter out the corresponding vibrational levels. By this we're able to categorize the different energy levels. So, these levels can be subdivided energetically, without there exists a spatiotemporally subdivision.

The vibration levels of our universe can now be roughly categorized into three parts:

1. **Spiritual levels (part of the unseen which is enabled to organize, to manage und to create).**
2. **More subtle levels (part of the unseen, which constitute quasi the aura of man).**
3. **Coarse level of matter (the visible which is the lowest energy level in the universe).**

The division into these three areas would have something to do with the aspects of body, soul and spirit. The hierarchical relationships then can be illustrated as follows:

Obove: ⬇   **Spiritual level(s)**
Below: **Physical level**

In between, roughly, the soul-subtle realm could be located (-> trinity-thought).

And to emphasize **the hierarchy**, we bring the trinity thoughts in the correct order: spirit, soul, body:
1. **Spiritual range of the Universe (top level(s) in the universe)**
2. **Soul-subtle area of the universe (middle level(s) in the universe)**
3. *Physical area of the universe (lowest level of the universe)*

Justification of the hierarchy and illustration:

1. **Spirit, who has the threads of the visible in the hands (like the theater Player of the puppet theater)**
2. **Subtle realm, which is quite the threads (like the threads of the dolls)**
3. **Physical area, which is represented by the dolls (the dolls are without the players only dead puppets)**

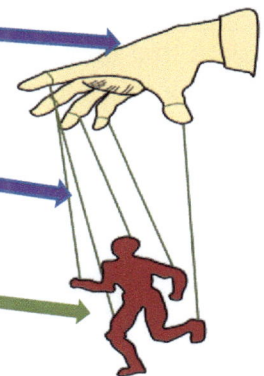

Because the levels of our world system towards the higher energy levels (or towards the centre of the bubble in the brane model) are becoming more and more fundamental, there is a clear hierarchy that marks the direction of the cause and effect arrow that points energetically downwards. Because these levels are present at every point in space-time, cause and effect are also present at the same time. So here we have no spatial-temporal separation from what is the cause and what is the effect, as is the case in the established models of science to date.

Accordingly, it is conceivable that as spirit, as illustrated in the sketch above, we have the strings of all events in our hands, albeit largely unconsciously. For the evidence that the spirit influences matter, see references 1-8 at the end of the book.

Further findings:

- The part of the invisible that is intelligent and has creator qualities is commonly called God or Spirit. In other countries this spirit is called Buddha, Allah, Brahma or other.
- So far, there has been a lot of belief that this spirit is something that is above or separate from us and that we ourselves are completely powerless.
- Since we are intelligent and are endowed with properties that have **something to do with creation, control, influencing or order**, we are also spirit by nature (kind of children of the Spirit or children of God). Reason: Children have to be like parents, because parents pass on the skills that they have, to their children. And so, the creator passes on the creator talent to his children.
- It should be clear to us that we are not as powerless as the religions and **sciences** have sometimes made us believe with their basic assumptions (**not spirit is the product of matter** but matter is the product of spirit).

- Our thoughts, feelings and convictions have more influence on our lives than we have been taught so far (placebo, nocebo, hypnosis phenomenon, epi-genetics, mental training, ...).

2. Energy follows the attention.

It is a spiritual principle that energy always follows our attention. This is simply because we are spiritual beings and because our thoughts are creative.

a. We are somewhere between HEAVEN (highest energy level) and Earth. This is comparable to a mixed water that consists of a mixture of hot and cold water. The mixed water takes a temperature in between. It is similar with us that we have bound our vibrations of thought to matter, but belong to the spirit that is at home in HEAVEN. Vibrations of matter are below (low). Vibrations of HEAVEN are above (high). And the vibrations of our being are in between.
b. Depending on attention, we remain bound to matter or we contribute to the liberation of our mind.
c. A few who have the system in hand want us to linger in mental dullness (mental entanglement) so that they can control us. On the one hand, they are lulling us to sleep with smartphones, television and other distractions and stir up fears for existence and fears of environmental disasters, climate change and pandemics (bird flu, swine flu, corona) on the other hand. They are responsible for ensuring that we are increasingly confronted with environmental toxins in food, electro-smog and other harmful radiation (5G) by making us believe that we need 5G and that herbicides and pesticides are the best alternatives in the fight against what appears to be destructive in the agricultural field. Instead of really striving for the good of the people, they are doing everything possible under a false guise (false flag) to restrict people's freedom as best they can. They do not tell you that you have self-healing powers and a certain basic protection due to your divinity.
d. Since we are spirit by nature and we can rise above all material laws, there are ways out of this dilemma.

e. The aim of this work is to show these ways.

In Chapter I, we talked about the fact that we always have only two choices in a way that we can act for life as well as against life. Depending on what we direct our attention to, we are energetically either pulled down or energetically lifted up. A path of forgiveness, of togetherness, of 'for-one-another', of faith, hope and love lifts us up. Because this path is at the same time in harmony with life, it gradually heals everything that has to do with any diseases and problems. The opposite path pulls us down, which comes with health problems and other problems.

3. The source of power.

In this study (see Volume 2 in particular), we clearly come to the conclusions that matter is a product of the intangible spirit. This alone is capable of control, creation and power.

> **We are all children of the intangible spirit.**
> **Because the intangible spirit is capable of creation,**
> **his children are also creators or capable of creation.**
> **What is creator, has power.**
> **So, we are not really passed out.**

At the moment it seems that it goes globally down the drain, so to speak. From a global perspective, it can be seen that this is not the case for everyone, because there are always people who experience an upward trend in their lives. This means that in principle it is possible for everyone, if they have common sense, to be able to oppose a general trend. The reason is that as children of the Spirit (children of God) we are capable of power.

4. What does it mean, to be a child of the Spirit?

So far, the established natural sciences have assumed that matter has emerged from nowhere and that earthly life has arisen from it at random. Accordingly, we are something like children of matter, and our mind must therefore be regarded as material.

In this study, we point out verifiable experiments that we humans have mental powers that influence matter. Further logical facts, which we provide in detail, indicate that our spirit cannot be material because matter in itself is not able to organize itself or to be able to influence another matter in a targeted manner. I provide valid arguments that matter emerged from something that we define as spirit. So, the spirit himself is not material. He is immaterial, and our mind belongs to the intangible spirit. More on this in Volume 2.

In the final consequence we have to demand (postulate) that matter cannot originate from nothing, but that it is a creation product of the spirit. So, we, who we belong to the spirit, are not children of matter but children of spirit. Western religions also speak of the children of God, and we also address the question of what God is or could be.

Question: If we are children of the spirit and therefore should also be capable of power, why do we only perceive our spiritual power / strength to a limited extent or sometimes not at all?

5. The power of thought.

Our spiritual powers always work, even if we are not aware of it. We can compare the mental powers of a person in conflict (unredeemed person) with a specific team of oxen. This team consists of two oxen, one pulling the front of a carriage and the other at the back. Enormous forces work, but in total they fall flat. The carriage does not budge, which gives the impression that there are no forces. It is the same with an entangled spirit who has in relation to a specific goal thoughts of two types: positive and negative thoughts.

The one kind of thoughts is directed towards this goal (one ox in front) and the other thoughts are directed in opposite to the goal (the other ox behind).

Dew-pulling

Barrow of Life

Worry about/of/...   **Thoughts about/of/ ...**
- disease,   - health
- deficiency,   - I can always have enough
- I must fight,   - we have mutual profit
- it does not work, because ...   - everything is possible
- ...   - ...

Remarks.
- Our conflicting attitudes, internal programs and believes tear us apart internally (internal division). Enormous powers act, but rather that our barrow of life can move forward, it is pulled back and forth.
- We are struggling, exhausted, frustrated and have ultimately achieved nothing.

Since we have a lot of ideas, we can also compare our thoughts with people involved in a tug of war game. As long as our thoughts, feelings, convictions, beliefs and the like are not in harmony with each other, they do not point in one direction of action but in two opposite directions of action, as follows:

a. If we observe our thoughts closely, there are negative thoughts as well as positive thoughts. Even if we try to think positively, we often cannot get rid of the negative thoughts. Seen in this way, there are thoughts in us that contribute to recovery and thoughts that contribute to illness. **It is then like the aforementioned tug-of-war game, where pulling is from two sides (there are great forces and yet nothing moves).**

b. With the placebo effect and in hypnosis, negative thoughts are largely eliminated, so that effects can be achieved here with no counterforce. **In the tug-of-war-game-metaphor this would correspond to the case where everyone pulls at one end (goes very easily in the desired direction).**

c. So, in order to help the mental level to work effectively, we have to work on our thoughts, feelings and attitudes.

We have been programmed for many generations,
- that we age
- that we have to die
- that we have to eat
- that this or that could harm us
- that we have to fight to assert ourselves
- that we are not given anything for free
- that we are powerless (in the sense that our thoughts have no power)
- ...

More programs during our upbringing:

- You have to do this or that in order to be lovable or a valuable person
- You are stupid, small, ugly, ...
- ...

All of these beliefs and programs work in us and are largely responsible for how the situations show us.

Basic problem: We still have no really clear view of the world and therefore do not know why things are the way they are. Accordingly, we are naturally torn in our opinions and beliefs.

Are there solutions? By allowing the possibility that we are the creators of our lives with our thoughts, feelings, visions, soul plans and convictions, it is conceivable that we have solutions to the dilemma. To do this, we have to bring all our thoughts into a targeted direction of action by creating a harmony with all our consciousness parts. It is pulling our barrow of life with all these parts in one direction (creating inner harmony).

Get the barrow of life going with ease

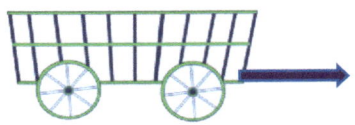

- **Swimming with the stream of life**
- **Way of trust, faith, hope and love**
- **Way of cooperation, of integration and of togetherness**
- **Investigating the inner impulses and intensions**
- **Following the inner plan**
- **Being in harmony with ourselves and the world**
- **Enjoying our life and potential of creation**
- **...**

Notes.
- **Thoughts, feelings, visions and goals are showing in the same direction.**
- **The hypnosis phenomenon is based on a certain programming. That allows us to be in a hypnotic state in which the mind, that would pull our barrow of life in the opposite direction, is turned off. In this state we have full speed, because there is no opposing force.**
- **A Life goal therefore might be, to free ourselves gradually from all negative and debilitating thoughts and thoughts of helplessness and struggle (using the above points).**

So, it's about focussing our thoughts - that is, concentrating. Any other thought that deviates from this concentration point (from the goal to which our thoughts are directed) usually counteracts the goal. The redeemed person then no longer has a single thought to doubt any goal he has (all of his thoughts, feelings, convictions and beliefs point in one direction). So, the goal is fulfilled instantly and without any effort.

The fact that more and more people are currently experiencing spiritual strength is due to the fact that these people are working to develop their abilities. Those who do nothing need not be surprised if their lives do not become easier. Instead, in order to assert themselves in this fast-moving and 'hard' time, they try to compensate for their lack of mental abilities through overexertion, struggle, hectic pace and stress. With this, they exhaust and finally resign because they hardly can do anything to their satisfaction. Then they are easily inclined to blame the outside, the circumstance, God or the devil or the world for their misery. They come into a vicious circle from which it seems that it is no longer possible to escape. Oh man, if you only knew that you were divine! Then you could save yourself a lot of effort, a lot of trouble and so many unsuccessful struggles.

The aim of this study is to show who or what we are and what is in our true power. The knowledge gained from this allows you to make yourself inde-pendent of everything and free. **However, there is a catch.** And this is that you can no longer hide behind anything or anyone. Because now you must not blame anyone else or anything else for your life other than yourself. After all, what happens to you is how it corresponds to your total conscious and subconscious thoughts. This is the analogy law 'like inside, so outside'.

6. The principle of power.

Based on the previous section 'The Power of Thoughts' we have seen that power has to do with the fact that as many thoughts as possible point in one direction. A person who is in harmony with all of the parts of his consciousness that he has can achieve goals with ease. However, such a person will not pursue goals that have anything to do with selfishness. Instead, he will only pursue goals that are conducive to the whole and that support the whole.

The fact, that the universe is how it is, is based on common ideas of all of us. As a result, it is shared by all of us. It is only because we have forgotten who we are that we feel as if we are sometimes very powerless and only in very small parts capable of the different levels of power. So, if there are people on earth who can influence events in the world very much, it is only because we consciously or unconsciously share their influence or support it in any form. **We consciously or unconsciously share or support their influence by letting us be frightened from them and thinking that we are powerless.** As long as we believe in our powerlessness, we will not oppose those in power and instead support their influence. Accordingly, this manifests itself on earth and we see ourselves dependent on them.

In reality, they are no more powerful than we are. In principle, we all have the same power.

Given the fact that there is a plan that leads us all into self-empowerment and liberation from all seemingly earthly dependencies, we can do the following to get into self-empowerment:

a) We always make it clear that it only happens to us according to our inner world of thoughts, feelings, ideas, visions, fears, sorrows and the like.

b) This means that we see everything that happens to us as the product of our inner world. Even if we are upset at first or let ourselves be frightened, shortly afterwards we keep reminding ourselves of point a) so as not to evoke further thoughts of fears, worries, revenge and the like (forgiveness).

c) We are aware that we can replace thoughts of fear, worry, revenge and the like with thoughts of trust, forgiveness and love. By favouring those thoughts and incorporating them more and more into our daily lives, we will automatically be confronted more and more with those things that fill us, that give us courage and that we can enjoy.

d) We are always ready to be guided by our higher guidance by trying to listen to our inner impulses and to trust them in a practical way (act accordingly).

e) We trust that we are well managed and that we are given the appropriate impulses in the state of trust, what is conducive to our progress and what leads to our self-empowerment.

f) We always intend to fit into our soul plan (explanation in volume 2) in such a way that we are always benevolent towards the whole and want to act accordingly.

g) By doing this, we can be sure that we will be provided with everything we need to serve this plan.

h) As long as we feel that not everything is being made available to us, the reason is that there are still any concerns, doubts or fears within us. It is precisely that by these things we still come across any situations that give the impression that something is in our way or that we are still passed out. Then we remember point a) again and proceed as described in the points b) to g).

i) We have achieved true power when nothing do longer mind and when we have fully relied on trust, what we can achieve step by step and bring to perfection. At the end of this empowerment process, we will be fully involved in the overall plan and will have the certainty of who or what we are (see Section IV.).

7. What are the deeper causes of the world problems and what solutions result from them?

- Our true essence is spirit, who is not subject to any separation. And spirit is light and love.
- Everything once fell out of the unit: It was the falling out from LIGHT from WHICH light (spirit) and shadow (matter) evolved, the shadow seeming to be as powerful as light (error).
- This led to the perception of separation and the oblivion of who we are in true essence.

- The idea of all of this lied in the fact that we have the possibility to perceive ourselves as a body with all facets, as we know them, separately from our spiritual awareness.
- This resulted also in a separation play (light-shadow play), where the perspective is different (instead of the spiritual view we have the view of the body, what has the consequence that things are turned upside down).
- The separation game has gripped the whole world, which means that it manifests itself on all levels (in large as in small, in all areas of life: economy, ecology, interpersonal relationships, ...)
- Although we have fallen out of unity, the knowledge of everything that defines our true nature has not really been lost. It is only dulled in memory. It is the knowledge of our true power, our integrity, our completeness, our true freedom and the like.
- Now is the time when everything is coming to a head and the effects of this separation game are becoming clearer, while the longing for what seems to be missing or what we thought was lost is growing.
- At the same time, this is the time when we understand better who we are and where we come from (time of real clearing up).
- And it is the time when more and more people are reaching their pain threshold that not only tells them that things cannot go on as before, but cries out for alternatives (**the real alternative to the materialistic world view is the spiritual world view!!!**)
- The increasing (separation) pain, which goes hand in hand with an increase in the longing for our true home, in connection with the motivation to get to know who we are, is suitable to initiate the change (turning back to unity) in practical manner.
- What we perceive from the perspective of the body must make us believe that a way out of the world situation described above is not possible. But if we go into the spiritual view, it is completely different. Then what we perceive is only the result of our wrong thinking, which we can correct (change).
- We are confronted with what we create in such a way that it becomes a self-regulating teaching unit that leads / forces us on the right paths and

ultimately let us wake up. We constantly compare our worldview and what we perceive. We judge things for correctness, sense, and the like, regardless of whether this judgment is correct. We are in constant dialogue and are constantly changing our minds. **As long as we are in conflict, in doubt, in search, in unrest, in strife and the like, this will not change. This dialogue only ends when we are again aware of who or what we really are.** Because then we are one with everything (in harmony) and in the state of perfect omniscience, perfect happiness, perfect security, perfect joy, perfect harmony and the like. But to get into this awareness, we need to rethink, that is accompanied by a change in behaviour (consistent with what we think and what we do).

- We can sum up the life teaching unit as follows: **Forgiveness knocks on our door until we see nothing in any more reason for struggle, dishonesty, hatred and deception.** As long as we didn't have forgiven we are confronted with death (in general: with illusions).
- The way back is the way from the I-feeling to we-feeling, from ego trip to the path for each other and with each other, from victim-thinking to self-empowerment, from lovelessness to love.

The goal is where it is possible,

- to gradually help people into their creative power so that everyone can recognize that they are the architect of their own fortunes with their thoughts, feelings and attitudes.
- to help these people to develop their natural self.
- to help them to become more and more confident.
- to help them to recognize their true calling / purpose.
- ...

8. The self-healing powers and the substantiation of alternative healing methods.

We know that everyone has self-healing powers and that healing can take place without any medication and without any outside help. The phenomenon of placebo and nocebo, as well as the knowledge of the ability to change our life in a targeted manner (power of thoughts, emotions, feelings and visions) are enough evidence to focus on self-healing. The so-called epigenetics, with which, among other things, the Saarland University deals with, provides very good approaches in this respect.

The deeper meaning of the term "medicament" is also interesting in this question. The word "medicament" is made up of the two terms "medicus" and "mens" (genitive form: mentis). "Medicus" is the Latin word for doctor and healer and "mens" is the Latin word for spirit and mind. See also the term 'mental` or 'mental power'.

Translated, medication means that the mind (spirit) is the actual doctor or healer and that the material aspect of any pill does not have a healing function. We are living energy. And living energy is never without influence. Therefore, for every symptom or problem of every human being there is a cause that needs to be found out. Two people who are in the same environment may face different symptoms or problems. Specifically, two people can carry the same bacteria or virus and still have different disease symptoms (one breaks out and other does not), which suggests that the individual symptom or problem has the individual cause and thus has to do with the individual human being. So, if someone is dealing with a certain symptom, the true cause of his symptom is to be found in himself or in his mental state. In other words, man's life situation always has to do with himself, so it is not a pure coincidence in materialistic sense.

Every person simply has a constantly lasting creative power through his energetic (being) and is therefore constantly influencing. From this knowledge it is deduced that everyone has self-healing powers and creative powers, which in principle allow him or her to be completely independent and free. Phenomena are also derived from this knowledge which, e.g. are known as placebo and nocebo.

Furthermore, the terms "medicament" and "medium" have the same stem. "Medium" is the Latin word for "middle". Seen in this way, we can also see the path to healing on the basis of this common root of words. It is the way to the centre or the way to connect with the deepest inside (the true centre in us).

In summary, the deeper meaning of the word "medicament" can be taken to mean that there is an inner healer (the real medicament) in every person who is capable of real healing. This healer has true wisdom that we can make useful by invocation or by connecting with him.

If we now look at the above-mentioned levels of being, we can see a certain hierarchy in the various disciplines in healing.

1. Spiritual healing (mental, Reiki, prayers, ...) is a discipline that is focussed on the spiritual realm. Thoughts / feelings / beliefs also belong to the spiritual level.
2. Homeopathy is the discipline that focuses on the subtle area via vibration (-> information). With acupuncture and acupressure, energetic impulses are given to subtle energy channels (meridians) in order to get energy flowing.
3. Classic medicine and naturopathy are disciplines that focus on the gross material plane.

Comments.
a) Meridians are known in acupuncture and acupressure, but cannot be determined directly in the classical biological sense (similar to invisible energy or invisible matter).

b) We always think about things, whether we eat, take medication or use other healing methods. In this respect there is nothing where we don't influence from the spiritual level at the same time.

c) Supposed contradictions in the success of the application can be explained by the placebo and nocebo effects as well as by the internal programs or believes, as already described above.

At this point it should be said that all disciplines in healing are justified. However, it should be made clear at which level they start. It should also be made clear that it is primarily a matter of finding and resolving the underlying causes of certain symptoms of illness in order to allow the self-healing powers to take effect. As long as these causes cannot be found and resolved, it often makes sense to resort to conventional or alternative methods to alleviate at least the symptoms.

Nevertheless, medicaments in pharmaceutical sense and/or applications or treatments, whatsoever, should always be viewed as a temporary aid until the client/ patient has recognized the real cause of his symptoms. Medicaments in pharmaceutical sense or particular applications or treatments cannot really heal. They can relieve symptoms at most. Real symptom resolution is only possible by the cause solution. If only symptom treatment is carried out - without cause solution - a symptom displacement is achieved with high probability, which is no real cure. Then it is launched a vicious spiral. This spiral can only be broken by a cause solution.

For more information on this section, please refer to my website:
https://franzguenterleicht.de/en/synergy-in-healing/

9. Our Self-empowerment.

The basic prerequisite for our self-empowerment is to be aware that our conscious, subconscious and unconscious thoughts together, which also include feelings, fears, concerns, worries but also visions and soul plans, create exactly what we are perceiving.

If we keep making ourselves aware of this and we pay attention to our inner impulses, this implicate that we let ourselves be less and less influenced by the external things. At the same time, this means that we no longer provide the breeding ground for fights, fears, worries and the like, which gradually makes us more confident.

It is also important to know that there is a plan for every being that allows it to free itself from the spiritual entanglement. This plan is known to our Higher Self. The Higher Self leads us out of this entanglement as we allow it to guide us. We can be sure of it if we surrender to its influence and let ourselves be inspired by it that it provides us with everything to be able to get out of the spiritual entanglement. By subordinating our minds to our Higher Self, in the sense that we ask it for advice and act according to its advice, which we receive in the form of intuition, inspiration, inner impulses and the like, we create an inner harmony. With this inner harmony, we have a creative power that points in a single direction of action, so that all the things we need on our way reach us with ease. Everything then happens for us as if by itself that way, we have inspirationally thought or wished from the heart or we have had a presentiment about it.

Of course, this is a process that does not necessarily end overnight. But we can always work towards completing it as soon as possible. How long this process takes depends on how much we engage in the guidance of our Higher Self and how much we can free ourselves from the spiritual entanglement.

Because the Higher Self is love, the more we engage in it, the more we are filled with love, confidence and gratitude. Likewise, in this process we will also see how things fit better and easier, which makes us more and more safe on our way. The more secure we feel, the less doubts, worries and fears arise. This relaxes us and brings us to inner peace. In relaxation and complete detachment, on the other hand, we are able to listen better to our intuition and our inner impulses and inspirations.

The path of letting oneself be guided, of forgiveness and trust, as just described, is the basic prerequisite for our self-empowerment. Building on this, it is important to deliberately deal with our thoughts. Yes, we can play with our thoughts and pretend that everything we picture is already there. The more we enjoy our thoughts and what we imagine, the more powerful we are.

For example, we can regularly take the time to send loving energies into the world and imagine how we live and how we want the world to be. We can also regularly take the time to imagine how we are surrounded by a protective shell that protects us from negative influences of any kind. Or / and we can imagine that we have a light-sword that always protects us from dangers and, if necessary, evicts or sends into banishing negative forces that tend to diminish our strength or torpedo our positive intentions. In addition, we can issue instructions that strengthen our power, as follows:

- *I [Your full Name] decree by virtue of my divine power, if any reprisals are imposed on me as a person due to an action on my part, if that action is motivated from my inner conviction and that does not violate the divine order, that this reprisal comes back to its author in such a way that he/she can no longer maintain it and that at the same time it evaporates into nothing. I am free.*
- *I decree that any radiation that is used against humans and nature is absorbed, neutralized and converted into healing energy by means of special filters that are set up in the morphogenetic field of the earth.*
- *I decree that everyone who is benevolent towards fellow human beings and nature and who would like to contribute to a new, livable, harmonious and freedom-developing way of life on earth will receive everything necessary for this.*
- *I decree that all influential people who (want to) oppose people's happiness in order to gain personal advantages will immediately be deprived of their influence.*
- *I decree that all people who have higher insight and wisdom and want to use this for the common good will have the appropriate power, strength and opportunity to be able to contribute optimally in this world.*

- *I decree that my soul is fully immersed in the field of light and the love of GOD and that at the same time my energy body system is adapted to the energy field of my soul.*
- *I decree that all is given to me (power, force and opportunity) that fully supports me in my mission to help the world.*
- *I decree that everything will be taken from me that prevents me from following my soul plan and carrying it out to the best of my conscience.*
- *I recommend putting my mind, my body, my ego, even my whole life, into the hands of GOD.*
- *I decree that according to this order presented here or a similar one, the heavenly powers are allowed to act here in this earthly process in the function of helpers, guides, advisers and protectors.*
- *I, who have inherited the creative power from GOD, decree that this decree is to be complied with now and that this happens immediately!*

This is how it happens. So be it. That's the way it is.

The more people find themselves who work on their self-empowerment and issue such decrees, the more those in power who want to subjugate people will lose their power, the more we contribute to the new earth. Let's do everything in our power to let come the new morning!

10. Conclusions from Chapter III.

Power always has to do with the fact that there are several people who share an idea together, because this means that the thoughts all point in one direction. The more are sharing an idea, the greater the power to realize that idea. We achieve greatest power when we fully integrate ourselves into the overall plan of God, which is borne by everyone, whether consciously or unconsciously.

This leads to the following saying: **"Together we are strong."**

IV. The power of the We-attitude.

1. The two basic attitudes.

Old basic attitude	New basic attitude
Everyone insists on their opinion and world view or thinks that they are right	Every opinion or point of view is important and contributes to enrichment
Focus on self-centered goals (greed, taking without giving or conditionally giving)	Focus on common goals (natural needs, harmonizing give and take)
Focus on lack	Focus on abundance
Selfishness	Focus on togetherness, unity
competitiveness, eccentricity, using the elbows	Strive for teamwork and collaboration
Economy without ecology	Economy in harmony with ecology
Limited, short-term and pure head thinking and the corresponding acting	Intuitive, horizon-opening thinking and acting, letting feelings speak

This basic attitude leads to
- Problems,
- Crises,
- Conflicts,
- Short-term success with a high expenditure of time and energy
- Unsatisfactory productivity
- Overexploitation of nature
- Ascent and descent
- Devil spirals

That basic attitude however leads to
- Solutions
- Pleasant being together
- Harmonious interaction
- Goals / achievements that are faster and easier to achieve
- Optimizing productivity
- Harmony with nature
- Sustainability
- Angel spirals

2. Requirements for success

Below is something about the prerequisites for success (in private, business and other areas) that sets in as if by itself, is quick and easy to achieve and can be sustainable (sustainable in the sense that the corresponding goal is to be pursued further and approved. So, in the event that a specific goal does no more want to be pursued, sustainability naturally stops):

a. Feeling of belonging (when everyone feels part of a certain community and can identify with this community or the idea behind this community).

b. Awareness of the own talents, skills and gifts, which everyone can best contribute to the community.

c. Mutual concession that everyone can and may participate individually according to their abilities, talents and gifts in such a way that it serves the community (family, company, state, etc.) in the best possible way. **Explanation:** What one is not good at, the other can do better. Because there are several things to do in a community, it is best for that community if the division of tasks is carried out in such a way that these individual skills, talents and gifts complement each other. Just as in a living organism every cell and every organ is assigned a specific task, in a community every individual can and should be assigned such a task that it can best do according to its talents, gifts and abilities.

d. Creation of a free-space within a given framework, which is given by the corresponding task to be performed in this community. **Explanation:** If a certain task is assigned to an individual within a given framework, it should be ensured that the individual can freely play a part in this task. Because the freer it feels, the more it enjoys its work and the better it can unfold.

e. To convey that everyone is a part of the community and that mutual profit is to be sought (what is good for the whole is good for every part of this whole).

f. It is optimal if everyone stands in the service of the community, no matter what position he is in, and if everyone respects and values the positions and tasks of the others!!!

g. In the position of a director, manager or supervisor, it is advantageous to be able to empathize with the concerns of the employees and when empathy, social competence, serenity and inner peace are strongly developed in him.

3. What is the aim of a society of the new time (keyword-like)?

- Create awareness of synergies for individuals and companies.
- Create awareness of spiritual principles.
- Create awareness for the knowledge that there is inner potential in every person that can be developed.
- Create awareness of a life of brotherhood (economic life), equality (legal life) and freedom (spiritual life).
- Create awareness of a society in which intellectual life (culture, education, religion, ...), legal life (politics, administrative law) and economy can manage themselves and follow their own functional principles relatively autonomously (social threefolding according to Rudolf Steiner's idea).
- Create enthusiasm for the big and the small things.
- Help to new experiences and knowledge (new point of views can contribute to new perspectives or reveal a new meaning in life).
- Arguments for a simpler yet successful life, whether private or business.
- Ideas for a more harmonious, easier and meaningful interaction of communities such as families, friendships, companies, that is, all types of associations.

The new Morning. It is time for man to take the next step in evolution. But he can do this only if he becomes aware of the spiritual laws (see Volume 2), if he realizes that his consciousness is part of an even greater spiritual organism and if he's ready at the same time to integrate himself into the hierarchical structure of this even greater spiritual organism.

In order to grow in this task, man can practice in all possible fields in which he is active. Practice is known to make the champion. For example, the insights into the principle of functioning of an organism can be applied to families, communities, companies and states. Even when it comes to international relations or geopolitical strategies, these insights can be used to lead humanity, which is also an organism, into a new era of brotherhood and freedom. Because behind each state is a kind of group spirit, who is equipped with special skills. Together, states complement each other, noting that there have always been epochs in which a nation or state stood out and advanced humanity in development, see [World Plan, Axel Burkart]. Nonetheless, every state (nation) has its legitimacy and mission to contribute to the new era (the new morning). Every state has to find out for itself its task.

Meanwhile, it is also possible for the mass to look more and more behind the scenes of this world events and to recognize the task of man (see Volume 2). This generally opens up the possibility that more and more people can contribute to the new evolutionary step at all levels, be it personal, business, national or international, be it in agriculture, medicine, environment or in any other areas.

4. Conclusion from Chapter IV.

The We-attitude provides the best prerequisites for achieving unlimited power.

V.   From unconsciousness (non-awareness) to awareness (from unconscious creator existence to conscious creativeness).

1. General Considerations.

Most of the thoughts that come to us come from imprints (inner programs) and habits. Accordingly, our response to certain situations is reactive. This means that we re-act similarly to similar situations because we are just used to it.

Unless we are aware of these re-active behaviours, we continue to act unconsciously and not necessarily the way we would like to behave, e.g. if we let our heart speak. Mechanical thinking prevents us from thinking independently. It prevents us from developing internally.

The advantage of mechanical re-active thinking and acting is that it is comfortable and we do not have to question anything. The downside is that we're not making any progress in terms of inner development and that things are repeating themselves, albeit in a slightly different form. We may think that there is always something new, but when it comes to true development, we are more or less at a standstill. It's like walking on a hamster wheel. Indeed, we move forward (on the wheel), but we are not really making any inner progress and cannot leave the cage (the limitation). **Mechanical thinking is contrary to our true nature, does not really satisfy us and leaves our desires unfulfilled.**

The disadvantage of non-reactive and transcendent (cross-border) thinking is that we have to check everything for correctness and consistency with the inner knowledge, which in the beginning seems a bit exhausting because it is contrary to our habit. We have to fight against the power of habit. The advantage is that we advance personally and spiritually and are able to gradually lift the boundaries of the mind. This process also empowers us and let us get to become more and more conscious creators. It corresponds to our innermost need. In this way we find ourselves and can satisfy our real longings.

The theoretical studies (see Volume 2) will show that we are all creators, whether we are aware of it or not. All of our thoughts, feelings, fears, inner convictions, visions and the like have an effect on everything we perceive. But mostly or often we perceive things that we do not like, that we are angry about, that make us afraid or worry. But they are all the consequences of our inner world of thoughts and feelings. This means that our creative power is completely undiminished.

If we cannot perceive this in this way, it is only because we are on the one hand unconscious creators and because we are on the other hand (still) torn, split or in spiritual entanglement, what we could see in Section II Point 5 (the power of thought).

As long as our thoughts and feelings are not in line with all our consciousness parts (consciousness, sub-consciousness, super-consciousness), we remain unconscious creators and always have any doubts about our creative power. **The only way to rise to the conscious creator is the way of letting being guided, the way of forgiveness, the way of trust, the way of listening to what our soul intends for us as well as the path of togetherness and 'for-each-other'.** There is a way for everyone to lead themselves to true self-empowerment. The Higher Self of every person knows this way. Therefore, if we want to become conscious creator we cannot avoid letting be guided and directed by our Higher Self.

Let us become an observer who learns to recognize more and more from what is happening to him, that this only has to do with himself!!! As a result, we gradually become aware of all unconscious thoughts, beliefs, visions, fears and the like. The more we become aware of all of this, the more confident we become. In the same way, the doubts that arise in us become less and less. At the end of this process, we become aware of all of our consciousness parts and become conscious creators. Then we can almost do everything we want from the heart, just as with the push of a button. We then will see that we want nothing more than to create something that is not only useful for us but also for the whole. Because this increases the joy, we will automatically participate in this increasing joy and will be even more motivated to create something that not only benefits us but also the whole. Then our life will find the highest fulfilment with minimal energy expenditure and maximum efficiency.

2. Conclusion from Chapter V.

The We-attitude in connection with the intention to fit into the guidance of our Higher Self provides the best prerequisites for becoming aware of who we really are.

VI. Transition to Volume 2.

In Volume 2 the current worldview - the materialistic worldview - is examined more closely with the result that we have to demand the existence of the spirit who is not material. If we take a closer look at matter, we come to the unequivocal result that it cannot exist, let alone is viable, without spirit.

Spirit is defined as living energy that is capable of directing, influencing, ordering, creating and abolishing. Since we are feeling and thinking beings, which are also able to influence, we belong to spirit and not to matter. Accordingly, matter is a purely creative product of the spirit.

How we are now to be seen in this overall context is discussed in detail in this volume. Have fun reading.

VII. Source/Literature.

1. Carpenter Effect:
   https://www.hypnoseausbildung-seminar.de/hypnoseinfo/hypnoselexikon/carpenter-effekt.html
2. Epigenetics: https://www.youtube.com/watch?v=HLJWj_hNki4
3. Epigenetics and others: https://www.youtube.com/watch?v=livLliVWWoY
4. PEAR - PSI Research at Princeton University, Influence of Mind on Machines: https://vimeo.com/4359545
5. https://www.amazon.com/The-Biology-of-Belief-ebook/dp/B001EQ5ZJK
6. https://www.consciouslifestylemag.com/mind-over-matter-experiments/
7. Plant experiment: Dr. Ing. Cleve Backster: https://dieter-broers.de/unsere-gedanken-sind-nicht-in-unserem-kopf-begrenzt/
8. Robot Chick Experiment:
   https://www.youtube.com/watch?v=M0cURvVvBew

Index